A MEDITATION ON

THE GOLD OF PLAYBACK THEATRE

A MEDITATION ON

THE GOLD OF PLAYBACK THEATRE

by

Annette Henne Rittenhouse

with a little help from my friend

Markus Huehn

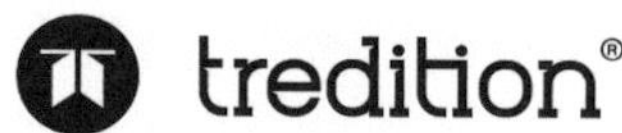

www.tredition.de

www.tredition.de
2014 Annette Henne
Auflage 1
Layout: Markus Huehn
Artwork: Mateo Schmitthenner
Verlag: tredition GmbH, Hamburg
ISBN: 978-3-8495-8048-3
Printed in Germany

Bibliografische Information der Deutschen Nationalbibliothek:

Die Deutsche Nationalbibliothek verzeichnet diese Publikation in der Deutschen Nationalbibliografie; detaillierte bibliografische Daten sind im Internet über

http://dnb.d-nb.de abrufbar.

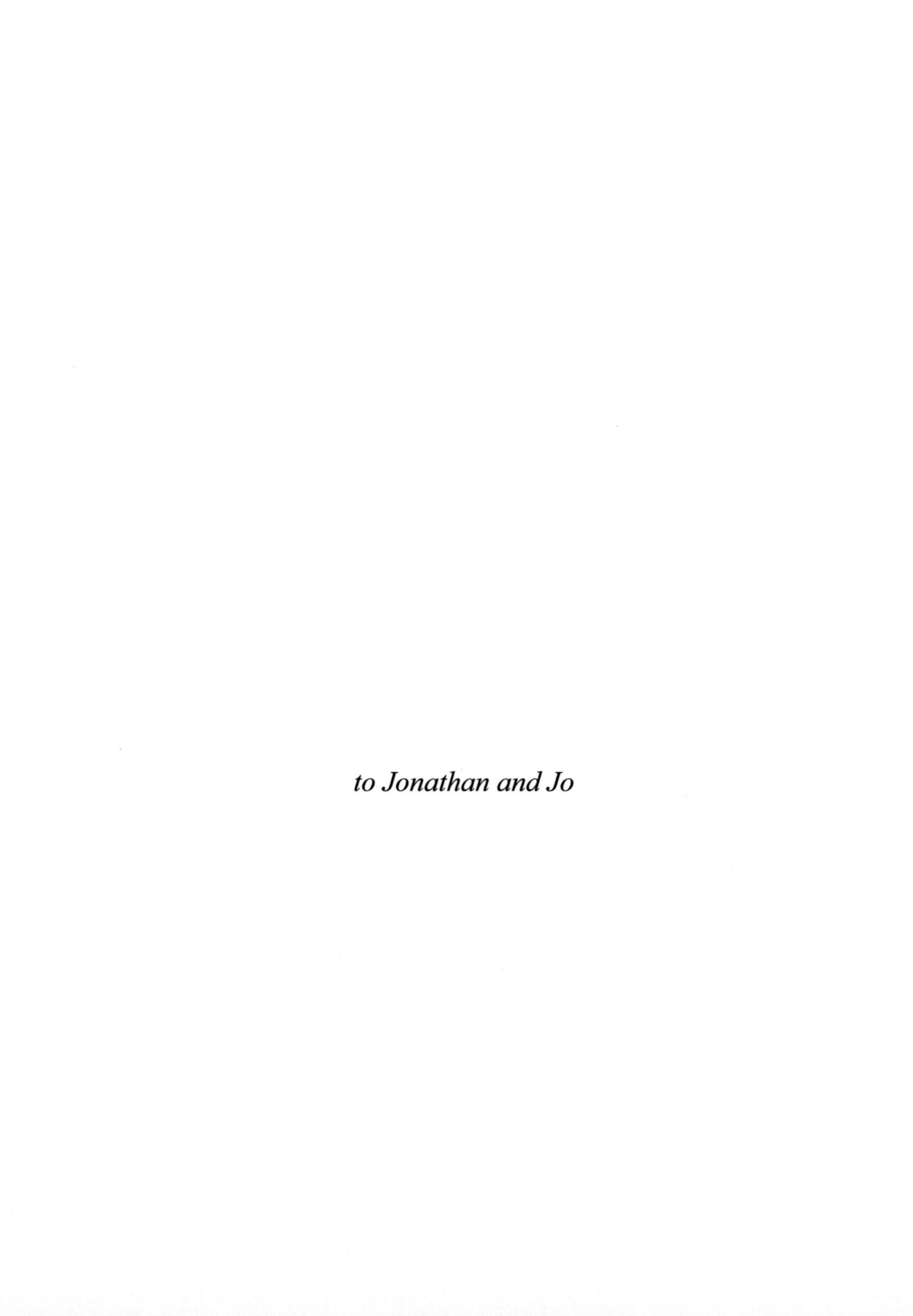

to Jonathan and Jo

Contents

Playback Theatre 9
Foreword 11
Introduction 14
A look at the beginnings 16
Theatre of Love 18
A common base 20

The Gold of Playback Theatre 24
Some Quotes on Basic Values 25

We all have a (worthwhile) story 27
Stories 28
You can't forget stories 31
The world we live in 36
The courage to be 40
A bond exists 46

As Community we are wise 51
Knowledge 54
Coherence 60
Community history 62

Everyone is a (creative) actor 65
Art 67
Three years old 73
Simultaneous dramaturgy 76

Community theatre 77
Eradication of blocks 79

Community spirit is transformational 87
Spontaneous participation 88
The first sentence 91
The benevolent mirror 92
The soap-bubble 94
The ritual 99
The frame of reality 99
The doors of magic 100
A love ethic 106

We can connect to a "music" 111
Celebration 120
Grace 122
Two-way contact 123
Day of fun 124
Dialogue 126
Creative zone 128

Afterword 132

The last story 135

The last candy 138

Structures in practise 138

References 150

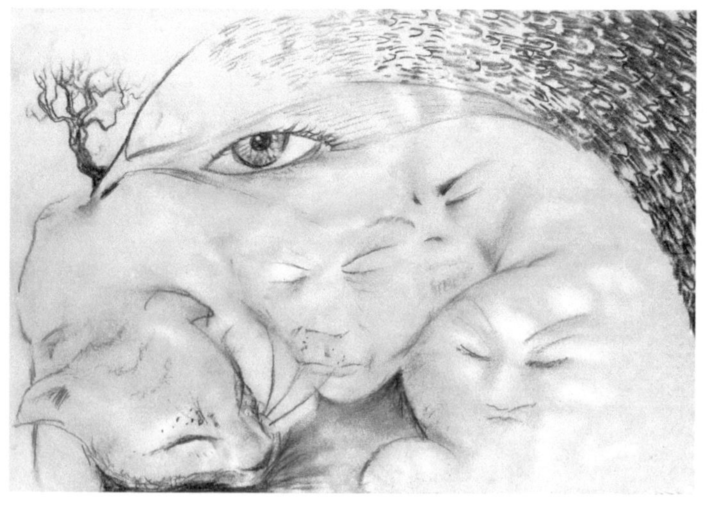

PLAYBACK THEATRE

Jonathan Fox of New York was born in 1943 and invented Playback Theatre in 1976 over a cup of coffee. He shaped all his ideas with the help of his wife, Jo Salas, and his friends (the original company). He established a theatre that fits no category, a theatre whose goal and impact surpass our imaginations.

The humility and sincerity of Jonathan's being are reflected in the stage presentation he created. Chairs in front seat the audience in curving rows with an aisle down the middle. Opposite, on the left, sit two chairs, slightly angled. Back in the middle (maybe also a little bit angled) are four or five wooden boxes for the actors. Further back and to the left sits a coat stand with a few colored clothes, and on the right side, in front of the stage, a few unique instruments. That is all. This stage is the same all over the world. From Japan to Africa, America to Europe, Australia to South America or Asia, if you see this setup, you know: Playback Theatre will take place here!

As profound and as loving Jonathan's being is, so is the content of this form of theatre. People are playing their personal stories to one another. As Jonathan says, "We enact what you tell. We accept any story on any subject. Every personal moment and every personal story of your life is worth a theatre piece."

Playback theatre is a special form of improvisational theatre. At the beginning of a performance nobody knows what will be performed, since the content of this theatre is made up of personal moments and stories from the people sitting in the audience. This not knowing is what connects everybody in the beginning. Parts and pieces from all layers of our existence are turned into short theatre pieces, played back in their essence by the actors and the musician without script or preparation. The conductor serves as a choreographer, a mediator between audience and actors, a "Shaman." The actors can take on five to twenty roles in one performance, only becoming themselves between roles, briefly. The musician has the crucial task of giving form and atmosphere to the theatre pieces. A space of magic and suspense, or a feeling of being deeply touched, opens up. What happens on stage is art. Art reflects the beauty and the clarity of a story. The stage becomes a space which allows access to all levels of life and of being human. Playback Theatre can impact people and society profoundly, because it is grounded in the concept of constructive change. Just as, in the beginning, the not-knowing connects people, the same people feel united at the end by knowing the ease and unease of living on this planet.

Playback Theatre is a little challenging for everybody: for the conductor, for the actors, for the musician, and for the audience. Nevertheless, it can be an experience that reverberates for some time, a theatre for the well-being of man, alone and together with others, an act of service for one another.

Welcome to Playback Theatre! Do you have a story to tell? For without you, the audience, there will be no Playback Theatre.

The conductor, the actor and the musician can be woman or man.

In the text we decided to write only "he", and no she/he or alternating gender. This has nothing to do with any preference of man, nor with any judgments. It simply is for the ease of reading.

FOREWORD

The more I know about Playback Theatre, the more I am fascinated by this unique form of theatre.

I first heard about Playback Theatre in 1986. I was attending a psychodrama workshop in England. On our last evening, during a candlelit storytelling circle, I mentioned to a friend from Australia: "It would be incredible if we could play these stories back to each other. That would be a new kind of theatre!" "Oh," she replied, "but this already exists: a man named Jonathan Fox in the United States is doing exactly that!" This is how everything started: from Switzerland to England, through Australia to America, and all around the world.

At that time, when I got to know Playback Theatre, there were no books about it, nor a school. At that time, when I got to know Playback Theatre, I was always on a search for more understanding of human beings and the world. With psychodrama, I had found an incredible treasure that allowed my inner child to play again. My being could be creative, inventive, and understanding. All parts of me were engaged. It was wonderful! Also I found the wisdom books of the Toltecs, which put into words all of what I felt and believed. A few years later, I found a medicine-teacher and a circle of people with whom I learned to open up in ways I never could have imagined. I got a glance into the richness of our consciousness and a further understanding of my being within the universe and being a part of creation. It brought me closer to what we may name "God," or also "That," because there is no name for it.

And last – but not least – I found Playback Theatre!

Playback Theatre is one of the most beautiful portals that opened up for me. My heart did not expect that much joy, that level of dynamic excitement and that kind of connectedness. It opened up dimensions which appear simply by playing back stories.

Everything concerning the life of human beings was included in a simple, but magical, way. Hope for a future with more joy and equality was not just talked about, but was put into action. We learned to grow up by playing like children, by delving into each others' lives carefully, as a loving mirror, and by experiencing the importance of the connection of the individual to the community by honesty and trust.

The many levels of Playback Theatre have been keeping me busy since the beginning. For this reason, I started to write a long time ago, and I got overwhelmed. I needed a "super-brain," and I found it. Not only did I find a wonderful friend, but also somebody whose spirit was on the same search as my own!

I met Markus Huehn at a German-speaking Playback Theatre meeting.

Since I was the one who brought Playback Theatre to German-speaking Europe, Markus wanted to interview me.

We immediately found ourselves sharing our ideas and our love for Playback Theatre, and an adventure began. We met for six weeks in Switzerland, working on what I had been writing and adding many new ideas. Finally, in 2003, our self-published German audiobook "Die Vision des Playback Theaters," ("The Vision of Playback Theatre") was complete. We planned to translate it into English, but that version never came out for various reasons. One of them was that I moved to Asia. But, it stayed in our heads all the time and we knew in our hearts: "We need to finish what has been started."

But, new material and new insights kept entering our heads. There was no way to just translate the German audiobook. We decided to focus our new book mainly on Jonathan's "Quotes." We had a new focus and also the wish to do it together.

Time passes – sometimes, faster than you realize. We tried to work together over the oceans, by Skype, by emails, and by short meetings in Europe or Asia. But, it was too difficult to write the book together. Markus was busy in Germany with all his creative projects – with Playback Theatre and his professional work – and had little spare time to write. I was in Bali, Indonesia. It gets dark early here. I started to fill my evenings and nights with writing. Sometimes I couldn't stop. I didn't stop. I didn't want to stop until most of what I had in mind was on paper. More than the audiobook, this book became like my "child."

Even though I wrote most of it on my own, without the support, the encouragement and the input from Markus, it truly wouldn't be what it is now. So, we decided to publish under my name, and "with a little help from my friend Markus Huehn."

INTRODUCTION

One page.

It was only one page.

Jonathan Fox handed me this page many years ago. We met in upstate New York in a small village for two hours, drinking tea and discussing my idea about writing a book with the title, "The Vision of Playback Theatre."

"I have something," Jonathan said, and handed me a paper. It was one page, with only a few sentences. This page had the title, "Some Quotes on Basic Values of Playback Theatre."

On this page were five main sentences representing basic values, and a few citations underneath each of them:

- **We all have a [worthwhile] story**
- **As a community we are wise**
- **Everyone is a [creative] actor**
- **Community spirit [and a mood of positive participation] is transformational**
- **We can connect to a "music" beyond our immediate concerns that will bring peace and joy**

Of course I wondered: What was the reason for noting just five sentences out of millions?

I thought each one must be really important. They must have a connection to one another, and for sure they express more than just a single phrase.

Furthermore, each sentence had a few citations underneath, out of books from different writers, coming from different parts of the world, writing about different subjects (psychology, sociology, theatre, philosophy, religion, and more). At the bottom of this page was one word like it had fallen down and gotten lost!

This made this paper even more suspicious and more important, and my curiosity increased.

It was the word "remembering."

What was it that must be remembered so it won't be lost?

Markus and I made it our very personal journey to explore and to understand the importance of those sentences for Playback Theatre itself: for its growth, for those who practice it, for all human beings concerned, and for the world the larger scenery involved.

How can we ever understand the world? There are so many different spaces and dimensions. Every human being lives in his or her own universe according to his or her consciousness. We never can compare or judge. We only can try to create beauty within our life with the spaces available in our momentary consciousness. We can enlarge our consciousness and gain more awareness. Our sense of self within the community carries the richness of growth. Playback Theatre highly contributes to this process.

"Some Quotes on Basic Values of Playback Theatre" are our magical wands, the gold to carry to all people. With them, more and more stars will pop up on a dark sky. We don't need to construct, by force, a milky way – it will develop in its own speed by itself. We just need to capture the values and apply them in a gesture of honesty, standing on the safe ground of their basic wisdom.

Having our roots grounded in the basic values and our wings of playfulness spread out, something magical can happen in our hearts. These basic values involve us in an evolutionary process we all are part of, and in which there is no shortcut.

The "Quotes on Basic Values of Playback Theatre" lead, step by step, from the personal to the transpersonal.

A LOOK AT THE BEGINNINGS

How does a wonderful theatre like Playback Theatre come into existence?

In each material consolidation and manifested form of the universe, or of the ordered cosmos, is an idea and its spiritual concept inherent, like the seed which already comprehends the significant characteristics of its evolutionary destiny. All important parts of its essence are already contained in it. No apple tree is ever going to have pears! The successful outcome of the form will be a clear mirror in substance of the indwelled idea.

Playback Theatre started with a thought and with a strong feeling.

The origin of the thought is called inspiration. It comes from deep within the heart and comes out as a vision.

When Jonathan Fox, as a young man, had this thought, it was the idea of an oral theatre without script. This theatre was different, new and reaching beyond. I think it was like a golden ball in his hands and he was very excited about it. It just was not so easy to put it 'on stage' to be what it was meant to be. But, his friends caught fire and they experienced the magic. That's what they wanted to reach: this magical level, which attained at the same time an ethical level.

The beginning was an experimental phase full of questions, full of fun: playing, trying and testing. They recorded every story told in writing to find out the dynamics, the background, and the best way to deal with narratives. It was nearly by chance, that music was added into Playback Theatre. Music opened up to a new space. Jo

Salas, Jonathan's life partner, deepened the magic of music in a wonderful way with her voice and her violin. Discovering music, brought in a new dimension, a transformative and deepening quality beyond words. Slowly, the "what exactly, and how," was gaining form and structure, and the first steps towards a system were set. But it was only years later, in 1986, that Jonathan committed his thoughts, ideas, and their meanings to paper in his first self-published book.

The awe we feel is often not so easy to explain at first. But, time has passed. Many things we already understand.

This one page with "Some Quotes on Basic Values of Playback Theatre" was like one more step. We found more explanation of what we wondered about, more answers about the "why?" and "what for?"

THEATRE OF LOVE

What a beautiful name for a theatre like Playback Theatre!

It is the title of Jonathan Fox's self-published book with the subtitle, "Dramatic Improvisation and Cultural Renewal."

The book's title shows what this theatre should be about: "...a theatre where the qualities of the heart matter most, which has a function for society and has a primary integrating force."

Playback Theatre is two-tracked, which means for the good of everybody (actors and audience), and also for the exchange of personal and transpersonal levels.

"Since Playback Theatre is process-oriented, there is a sense of something 'soft' about Playback Theatre's concept," Jonathan writes. "We are nurturing, caring, concerned to create beneficent atmospheres, while the 'world' we mostly live in values more traditionally masculine rubrics."

Since normal theatre is hierarchical, self-indulgent, proud, and competing, Jonathan Fox wanted a theatre that is directly concerned with social needs. He wanted to create a theatre that is intimate, personal, communal, and also intense, but ultimately a "theatre of love."

Jonathan's primary concern was that, "Playback Theatre should be a community theatre, where it is possible to tell all kinds of stories. In a community theatre there will be memories that tie us to the past and also turn us toward the future as a community of hope."

It has a context which allows us to connect our aspirations with those of a larger whole and see our own efforts as being, in part, contributions to a common good.

"The richness which is shown in stories kicks us out of our sleeping consciousness, where we drift from experience to experience,"

Jonathan continues. "It makes us more capable persons. Stories are a treasure hoard of wisdom and fun, and connect us to others."

Playback Theatre is an improvisational theatre, which, to Jonathan Fox, means: "...both a practicing ground for life and an arena for exploring further dimensions of mind. Through it we can leap beyond the limitations of our frames of living, risking chaos to find order, daring not to think, to achieve higher understanding, attempting to be both in the moment – so that our inhibitory observer is silenced – and out of it, benefiting from meta-level perspective."

This leads us to spontaneity, "that flow of sensory information, evaluation and action that fuels our ability to adapt with creativity to a constantly changing environment. Our lives consist of a mammoth improvisation, in which each moment is a spontaneity test!"

Theatre can be a strong force for preserving social ecology, the "web of moral understanding," and commitments that tie people together. Playback Theatre can transform individual lives and help people to form a real community.

Through sharing our experiences and by telling our stories in Playback Theatre, we can sense better our needs and this can help us to find new hope, to overcome our fears and to accept our not being perfect. It can be a way to overcome boundaries of different cultures and bring an understanding for all the different ways to live life.

The content of Jonathan's first book is a precious gift. After more than 35 years, there is no better way to put into words what Playback Theatre's meaning and goal is: to inspire people towards new visions.

Playback Theatre turns its view towards a "community of hope," with a context that is meaningful and allows us to get in touch with a wider view of the whole. It entails the future, involves the joy and the suffering of the present, and contains the beauty of our origin.

A COMMON BASE

How beautiful it is to tell your moment or story to somebody who is listening! How releasing it can be to be captured by what you have been telling! How amazing it is to see your moment or story unfold on stage as a piece of theatre, which is a mirror of what you really felt and experienced! How exciting it is, to play back somebody's moment or story and see a kind of tension in the teller's face changing into a "yes" from his heart! I could add many more "hows!"

To capture and bring the real value of Playback Theatre to the world, we need common ground. We need knowledge about the vision and the mission.

In 1990, the International Playback Theatre Network (IPTN) was founded. We were only a few people from different countries. It was a big step, an opening to the world and a clear verbalization of our vision and mission.

The Vision

People engaged in Playback Theatre embrace the unfolding of life and the inherent spontaneity of persons and communities within their own cultural, social and political contexts. We recognize the universal longing for affirmation and for connection with others. The spontaneous enactment of personal experience, the essence of Playback Theatre, builds connection between people by honoring the dignity, drama, and universality of their stories.

The Mission

The mission of the IPTN is to facilitate connections among people practicing Playback Theatre, to support the development of

Playback Theatre worldwide, and to promote shared ethics and values in the global playback community.

For a long time, Jonathan Fox hesitated to put the idea of Playback Theatre into a system, which would include protecting the name and forming the foundation for a school.

It was a real dilemma: on one side was the wish to encourage everybody, everywhere; and on the other side was the knowledge that the idea must be taken seriously and understood for it to be called Playback Theatre. On one side was the need for structure, and on the other side were the restrictions that come along with it.

We had many talks about it. Establishing a school would mean putting something into a frame which originally wanted to release frames. It would mean to structure something that, from the concept of spontaneity, cannot be structured. It would mean to judge, while the idea was non-judgmental. But Playback Theatre was expanding fast and training became necessary. In 1993 the School of Playback Theatre was founded by Jonathan Fox. Playback Theatre got its name approved and became the unique theatre it is.

It was not an easy task to turn the efforts to this direction. And, it still isn't an easy task!

There were many questions: what criteria do we set to call a playbacker a playbacker, and how do we bring them vividly into the learning process? What structure do we create, which steps to take? How do we teach that the values are not only meant for a small circle, but are also meaningful to very different countries and cultures? How can we bring the vision to each heart so that the hearts of all playbackers are pulsing towards the same understanding?

Playback Theatre by now has grown all over the world, which brings new and challenging subjects to its development. This was for example addressed in the theme of the 2011 IPTN Conference in Germany: "Sozialer Dialog in einer Welt des Umbruchs," or "Social dialogue in a world of upheaval."

A world of upheaval? This seems a very broad subject.

Upheaval is more than something in the midst of change. It touches the whole world: societies, cultures, and all the human beings living within those structures. Playback Theatre will have its special place in the process of upheaval in this world. The challenge for us playbackers gets bigger, because we need more than ever to represent the valuable gift of Playback Theatre, using dialogue in a very specific way on stage. For this, we must know what we are doing and keep our clear focus. For this we need dialogue with one another about how to pass on the value of Playback Theatre in the right way.

Playbackers all over the world are more than ever confronted with social and global disorder in our world, and also with subjects that surpass local matters and belong to a larger scope. We need to be ready to go along with the changes and we have to be careful to pass on the real gold (and not a faked one) which was put in our hands.

By exploring the quotes Jonathan Fox provided more deeply, we saw so many more levels showing up. There were so many more connections of different subjects appearing.

It was often not so easy to express what we discovered, because verbalizing what in some way is not really explainable, seemed sometimes impossible and sometimes even stupid. There is something that lies beyond words, defying explanation and beyond the scope of our mental concepts.

It was a journey into the known and into the unknown, and it became an adventure which was fulfilling and fascinating!

We found it ultimately important not to forget our roots while contributing Playback Theatre to the world. If we have a common focus, I believe we can step forward together easier. We are better able to communicate without getting caught in the limitations of our own, local structures and individual drives, and we are better able to accept the diversity of different cultures. The deep value of Playback Theatre can reach a magical level we all want to reach, no matter which company we are in – no matter which country we are in. It is something basic. It can be a shining star on a dark sky, a golden ball we pass on, or maybe more than a drop of clear water for a challenged world and its frequently disturbed inhabitants.

"Some Quotes on Basic Values of Playback Theatre" can help us to stand on common ground in the growing movement of Playback Theatre and can be a common understanding of our work. It can keep us connected, loving and competent.

This book is for "remembering."

It has its focus on basic wisdom. Those five sentences with their citations may lead us to a new understanding of Playback Theatre. To capture Playback Theatre means to capture the many levels and dimensions of human relationships and lives within the world.

THE GOLD OF PLAYBACK THEATRE

The basic values of Playback Theatre involve us in an evolutionary process we all are part of and through which there is no shortcut. As in all processes, there are steps to take. They have an inner connection to each other, and their building-up means there is no chance to leave out one part. It is like building stairs. The construction will only be safe for human beings when the foundation is solid. The stairs lead to something valuable, to something human beings are longing for, to something to live for – to meaning in our lives.

The basic values lead step by step from the personal to the transpersonal. To put it in other words: the basic values take us from the worthwhile individual life to the importance of all, and finally, to the interconnectedness of all life.

Playback Theatre is no therapy and is not meant as therapy – Playback Theatre is theatre! But from the point of view of its impact, we clearly will see its therapeutic and healing potential and effects.

Playback Theatre shows a possibility, through individual experiences of "real" life played back on stage as improvisation, to be in this world with a heart that is connected to the whole world and to contribute to an existence with more joy and in congruence with an infinite energy flow.

SOME QUOTES ON BASIC VALUES OF PLAYBACK THEATRE

It is our wish to share with all of you the truth, the beauty and the seriousness we find within those quotes.

The best way to do this is by taking you on a journey; a journey on which you can join our thoughts, discoveries, feelings, our heartbeats and our outcomes.

On this journey we will stop at different points of interest. It's like we would stop to look at a beautiful flower; to sit on a bench in the sun; to explore a stone on our way; to find a hidden cave; to stand still in awe of a star; or mostly to discover something precious.

In short, we may take smaller or bigger detours, but we will always have our focus in mind to stay on the chosen track. We will "meditate" on each quote and it's specific citations.

We also would like to encourage you, to not just read what we are putting in words, but to take your time to find your own images or words by following our meditation. Your journey will than be an unanticipated enrichment and personal gain.

WE ALL HAVE A (WORTHWHILE) STORY

Let's already stop here and have a closer look at these words and what they express:

We all have a story.

We have a life story called biography.

The expression "we all" is an important basic statement. It's not just "everybody!"

"We" is more private, more directed to something in common and also expresses connection. It is the "we" we are seeking in Playback Theatre, and to reach this "we," we need to pass through the personal "me:" the individual, the personal story.

"We" is inclusive.

Playback Theatre is inclusive.

"All" means all human beings on Earth, each one of us.

All are welcome in Playback Theatre.

Worthwhile is put in parentheses, which gives this word a special importance.

We all have a worthwhile life.

"Worthwhile" is no judgment; it is just a statement.

Stories are our connecting part. They are our experiences and our starting point in Playback Theatre!

Since stories have so much importance, we want to take some time to explore their meaning.

Stories

Stories are the outcome of our experiences. They are our way we handle this life, our way we struggle in life, and all the other beautiful experiences we can have in life! Every experience is just what it is: maybe good, maybe bad. But, it is an experience and can become a story. Those experiences express all of what it means to be human, a manifested spirit on this earth and having no other way than living in this particular form and traveling the road which is presented to us.

Every human being is served with different experiences on his or her plate in life, and for that, life is really interesting and rich. On this plate are many different tastes: some sour, some sharp, some sweet – many, many different tastes. All of those flavors make life! If we would stop to judge them, we could find out that they all are delicious. All are part of our life, and if we look at them from this perspective, they all are special in their own way!

Our stories are like our most personal pattern, our individually woven imprint made up of millions of personal moments. We are going through life, and the pattern is woven from the very beginning of our existence.

The story we are going to share below contains many layers of subjects and feelings: having courage for something we have been afraid of, the uncertain outcome in a foreign country and culture, guilt-feelings, the fear of punishment, the release, the importance of not being alone, somebody who can calm us and, last but not least, a "happy end." Where does this story have its origin? We don't know. Why was it told? We don't know. In Playback Theatre we don't need to know. It is the truth and there is a reason for it to be told.

Monica, a German woman, staying in Bali for some time, already had become accustomed to the Balinese traffic, but until now she didn't have the courage to drive herself.

"Me and the driver drove through the lovely landscape and some villages and I got the impulse to drive myself. We changed places and I was driving slowly, and it was a lot of fun! But suddenly a chicken ran with a lot of noise towards the car – and under it. I stopped immediately – but it was too late, the chicken was dead. This happens hardly ever, because chicken grow up on the road! I felt very bad. I was nervous and shaky. What kind of trouble will come out of this? But the driver only laughed, saying: 'No problem, don't be anxious, no worry – the family will be happy to have chicken for dinner tonight!' I was so released and a burden fell from my heart."

The audience had a lot of fun watching the actor as chicken running under the car, laying dead with his legs straight up.

Jonathan Fox mentions: "People need to tell their stories. It's a basic human imperative. Playback Theatre reaches down to the deep, undying need for connection: to be worthwhile, to be heard, to be affirmed and welcomed as one who shares the human condition."

Yes, I have a story – yes, I exist!

Stories are the proof of being alive, of our existence, of being within life. Being alive is basically a worthwhile fact! Playback Theatre values life and the experience of human beings who are living on this planet. This is our inner attitude towards stories.

If we have a worthwhile story, we are worthwhile beings. But, we don't always feel like that.

We keep ourselves busy doing things that we must do to feel worthwhile.

Most people define their worth only by their work. Deep within, there is this "judging voice," which tells us that we are not worthwhile for one reason or another. It always finds some reason. We learn to listen to it carefully, and we even believe it.

Tina, on the tellers chair, expressed that she feels absolutely useless. She fell ill with a nerve disease. Most of the thirty people in the audience had the same or a similar disease. The other people in the audience were family members or supported them in their life. The feelings of being worthless, small and helpless touched many others in the audience. Before that sickness Tina loved rowing, which she never will be able to do again. But now she is the trainer of the youngsters, she told on the tellers chair. Every day she needs some help to move from her flat to the training sessions. The parents of the children are offering her help by giving her a lift, but Tina has a hard time accepting this offer.

"I don't want help from anyone. I have nothing to give back in my life," she explained. "The only thing what I want is to bring joy to the children, but I can't do that anymore." Some sentences later, she told the audience that the children are so happy when she arrives at the center.

Seeing her story on stage, Tina saw glimpses of the gift she is bringing to those children. She felt released and with a glance of hope and a little more self-confidence she went back into the audience.

The first citation within quote one brings forth different aspects of stories.

"You can't forget the stories, and you think about them not only here, when we're talking about them, but in your car, or when you're walking, or when you're out there doing your work."
Coles, The Call of Stories, 1989

Do you tell yourself stories? We all do! We tell ourselves stories of what we have done, who we are, what needs to change or to stay the same, and what is wrong. We tell stories of freedom, bondage, grief, joy, longing; stories about someone else. Our experiences leave traces, and what has left traces, we are going to tell ourselves in a new way again – remembering the past and projecting it into the future. Thinking means to talk to yourself.

Our mind is always busy with some stories. In some way, most people are caught in their stories! They jump around in our mind.

Scientists say that we have about 60,000 thoughts per day. Whatever I am telling myself, horrible or grand, is often a distillate of experiences.

Our experiences have an inner connection. Experiences get connected in different ways and are fitted into former experiences, even they don't really fit.

We make another stop here: If we take a glance at Neurobiology, we get to know that the most complex organ in our body is the brain and the nervous system – an extremely complex, sophisticated network of cells which is responsible for making us human. The brain controls all our movements, perception, feelings and innermost thoughts and memories. All information has been stored through senses (taste, touch, smell, hearing, sight). Series of disconnected fragments which do not have a meaning by themselves are remembered by association. Memory is the glue that binds our mental life together. Our memory is a mixture of particles we accepted or rejected.

At the end a story is like a personal being, connected to the world in a special way. If we have a specific memory, we remember special events in our life and they are, in their own way, connected to other events. Therefore, we have our individual memory and our individual kind of stories.

The lived experience of an event involves the context of the event with past experiences and categories of interpretation, the impact of the event itself as you live through it, and its effect on the future possibilities of experience and interpretation. Happenings in our life get connected – or contaminated – and therefore most of our experiences are past, present and future at the same time.

A story told is not only connected to the whole life story of a person, but also to other human lives, society, culture, humanity itself and in the end, to the Universe. There is no isolated experience!

We don't think about a story as a whole one. A story never has a complete, rounded shape. A moment – our reaction in form of a feeling – is the kernel or the starting point. The story is an event put in a frame.

Since 'a story' (as something separated, isolated, with a clear form) doesn't exist, a story tells about something which, conscious or not, has some importance in a teller's life. Playback Theatre puts the story in the 'here and now.' What is told on the teller's chair is a condensation of the event which consists of many different moments. It is the conductor's job to lead the teller through and to the core of his experience so it can become a story with a beginning and an end. A story has a beginning, when we start telling it. In Playback Theatre this normally set by the conductor's question "When did your story happen?" and/or "Where did your story take place?"

With those questions, we bring the story in the 'now;' we set the first part of the frame and enter into its reality. With the guidance of the conductor it takes form, gets filled with emotions, and must have an end. A story – which didn't have a clear shape before, with a kernel of somebody's experience – now has the perfect form for the actors to play back a piece of life, a piece of theatre, a piece of art.

How exciting! What is going to be shown on stage? How is the story going to be picked up and played back? What will be the next 'now?'

But we are already jumping too far ahead of ourselves!

So let us simply come back to the first quote and to our citation.

Yes, we think about our stories – stories are vivid beings with many shapes!

To think about stories is one thing. To tell a story is another thing! And to tell a story in Playback Theatre is definitely a different thing!

In daily life it normally happens that stories are 'thrown at the feet' of somebody else. Most people don't ask if the other person is willing to hear what we have to tell. We just want to tell, to get it out, to unload or reload! What we rarely do with our stories is tell them to someone we know is listening and wants to hear them.

I am personally very fond of some American Indian traditions, because they are full of beauty and wisdom. There is one special teaching I remember well.

In one Indian tribe it is a normal habit that, before entering a house, you place your sorrows, joys, and stories in a basket, which hangs outside by the front door. You don't just fall with your baggage in the middle of someone's home; you aren't placing your story in the center of the room and occupying it. You wait for your moment, for the time your story will be heard. In this moment you will know that you are invited to bring your story inside and that it is time to share. Then your hosts will listen for sure and take part in your life. That's a wonderful habit. It is the way moments and stories are told in Playback Theatre!

In Playback Theatre you are not just telling something. You will be asked and you know you will be listened to! There is a space where individuality can be shown and is looked at as a gift!

Being asked to tell a personal story in Playback Theatre is an unusual invitation for a public or private performance. This starting position has a very different platform, and it initiates excitement and some tension. This makes Playback Theatre special, because our starting point leads directly to the heart of life. We introduce another way to open up connections between people and to look at what it means to be human.

Listening is another task in Playback Theatre.

Listening is an activity, not a passive "letting it happen." We have to listen attentively to what the teller expresses with words, with more comprehensive signs of the body and in his voice. We are alert and observant of our own reactions in mind, body and emotions.

In Playback Theatre, I listen to your story in a respectful way, because you have a worthwhile story. We want to know about your experiences. We are curious to get to know your special story, your uniqueness – and we want to play it back to you. You tell a story. Nobody else can tell this story the way you do. It's your personal experience and you are putting it in your own words. It's like nothing that's ever been before, and there will never be anything like it again. It's an original.

Of course there are people who come with a prepared story or a story they already have been telling, even a few times. There must be a need for it. But most people tell the most interesting stories. There's nothing worse than a second-hand story! Second-hand stories usually become jokes. First-hand stories always carry a certain magic, because it's the gift of the unique experience to others – and to ourselves. To tell a personal experience in Playback Theatre, you must raise your hand and share it with many. You may be asked to come on stage on the teller's chair. The spotlight is shining on you and for a while you are the center of attention! For this reason we believe that the stories told in Playback Theatre are always special and significant – even they are just an ordinary moment of daily life. And more than that and even more important: you know that this story will be played back to you. It will become a piece of theatre. It will become a common experience! All people take part in some way in a piece of your life, and you take part in your own story as a watcher and a participant.

This can change our perception. We might find a new meaning or a solution. This is also valid for others watching our story.

In Playback Theatre, we are not dealing with written theatre pieces, but only with personal experiences as told. Our theatre pieces are directly connected to the lives of the human beings present in this moment, in this performance. This makes every teller and every story special. This makes each actor and each team unique. And it makes every performance incomparable.

The world we live in

We are wonderful creatures, but also the funniest of all species. Humans are born with a very special awareness. They are the only being with consciousness.

But, we rarely apply this consciousness in our lives. It is said that half of humanity thinks about things that do not matter to them. That creates an enormous pressure. It is one of the great conditioning forces in the way humanity conceptualizes. Our mind is filled up with rules and laws and thousands of unimportant thoughts. The world is full of duty, of musts and expectations, and seems unfair. We have lost touch with our innate sense of genuine fun and lasting joy. We have to work hard to be accepted, because we have not learned to respect or love ourselves.

The world we are living in is no paradise. Many people feel that we live in a crazy world. We can even be more clear and think of it as kind of a mental hospital!

We are living in different societies, in different countries, in different cultures. We therefore have different experiences – but still we all are human beings!

Humans on this earth are, in fact, very special and by nature, very sensitive beings.

We are emotional, because we perceive everything with our emotional body. But we have this disease, a 'virus' like a computer virus, which has infected our mind. The disease has the name 'fear.' We are afraid to get emotionally hurt and need to protect ourselves and wear social masks. The result of this disease is the emotions that make us suffer, and manifested as hate, anger, jealousy, envy and many more. It is emotional poison.

"My neighbor, a paddy farmer, created objects against the birds eating the rice out of Coca-Cola cans and a stick. They made an ear-battering, irregular noise when the wind was blowing. Not only one, but many – day and night there was hammering and clipping and it seemed like a torture not to know when it starts and when it ends! I couldn't sleep anymore. There are no birds at night! Asking him to reduce this noise and to please take them down at least at night or to find another solution against the birds like the other farmers – he even created more! I began thinking about something which will get really on his nerves and will disturb him the same way (or better: worse). Being aware of my emotional poison, which just wanted to give back and harm, I decided not to choose this direction, but to ask him what he needed and wanted to solve my problem. He wanted me to cut all the trees down to three meters, which were giving shade to his paddy. I did. He reduced his orchestra to one object – which is still disturbing me! I still feel angry and powerless about his hostility."

I told this story in a small performance for friends. The teller's actor got even more furious than me, which was releasing. But, I clearly saw how my emotional poison and my anger switched into being mean.

Emotional poison is seen everywhere in our system, in our behavior in the world and in the way we connect and live in our relationships.

The world becomes a place of war and violence, a place of punishment that never ends, a place of judgment and no real justice. People are full of blame about themselves and others.

For thousands of years this disease has already been in this world. Psychiatry books, psychology books and medical books don't describe this virus or this disease as abnormal. They consider it normal. But, for sure: it is not!

Each of us human beings creates a personal dream for our own self, and with it, we disconnect from others. There is also a big outside dream, the dream of human society created by all the humans before. The outside dream is the collective dream of billions of dreamers and includes all the rules of society, its laws, its religions, its different cultures, and ways to be: The "Dream of the Planet." All this information is stored inside the human mind.

The normal world is filled with human beings who are in some way deeply disturbed or frustrated. They are disturbed because they are no longer connected to their unique life force. They are always trying to accommodate, fit in, work with, and be like what they're not. The mind-driven egotism is evident in our conformist yet competitive modern societies. Survival and security are just by-products: we must belong and fit into the system to get them.

We live our life as well as we can – normally, like everybody else. We eat the same stuff as the others eat, we work the same way as everybody else does, we start and end relationships like anyone else. In short, we seem so incredibly similar to one another. At the same time a phenomenon occurs which says that, if many people do and believe the same, it seems to be proof of its rightness. At the end we trust that what is right for others is also right for us, and we belong to the crowd. To belong is nice: we don't need to explain ourselves and don't feel pressure.

We have not been educated to be unique, and most of our spontaneity and creativity is fast put in the background. There is an ignorance of our inborn right to be ourselves and to be connected in depth. We don't really know who we are and who other people are.

How quickly that originality of perfection, as it comes out of the womb, is immediately conditioned, immediately smothered. Conditioned by the way it is communicated to, the way it's fed, the way it will be educated, the way it will be trained to use its mind to run its life, that treasure of originality gets lost.

The real 'Us' is pure love – we are 'life itself.' It has nothing to do with the big outside dream. When we see the dream from this perspective, and if we have the awareness of what we really are, we see the nonsense behavior of humans. But we have no choice. The voice in the mind keeps us from seeing what we really are. We are born in this society, we grow up in this society, and we learn to be like everyone else.

We have to be aware that these people of this world we just tried to describe, are the humans who are telling their personal moments and stories in Playback Theatre!

With the same awareness we also can see the impact of Playback Theatre's vision and concept.

The world could be a paradise.

What if there was a cure for this illness?

We would have no more wounds in our emotional body. We would live on a planet where every person has a different kind of emotional mind. We would no longer be afraid to be who we are. Whatever somebody would say about us or anybody else, we wouldn't take it personally. It wouldn't hurt anymore. It would not be dangerous to open our heart, to love, to share, because we wouldn't need to protect ourselves. We could experience and express in our unique conceptualization. It is the way in which all of us, in a sense, are intended to be able to communicate with each other. We are here to interact and communicate in a way that is honest and in a way in which the mind gets to display its true gifts. The universe has given each one of us sort of a unique nucleus, because it needs each one of us the way we are! It needs exactly this special part.

Our attitude "We all have a worthwhile story," can already make a difference in the world.

"The courage to be is the courage to accept oneself as accepted in spite of being unacceptable." Tillich, The Courage to Be, 1952

This is another citation below the first quote.

Acceptance seems to me one of the most important themes.

We need to be conscious, that 'to be' needs courage in our world.

It is the base of being worthwhile.

I like the following description of courage, because it 'encourages' us to not give up to where our heart wants to go:

"What is really needed for courage is hope in the most impossible situations, and endurance in the most adverse circumstances!"

In The Courage To Be, Tillich states that, "courage is the strength to continue to live on in a meaningful way in spite of the fact that our existence appears to have no purpose. We do not wallow in doubt, self-derision or despair. We have come into being in this time, in this place, in spite of the ever-present threat of the 'non-being'".

Tillich is referring to, "the underlying but nagging realization most of us suffer briefly – or for a lifetime – that existence has no purpose." We come into being at birth, then learn through daily life experience that death, nothingness, non-being awaits us. Rather than fighting this life, it could be that we can experience its pleasures. The courage we need is to accept our utter finality and that we are going to die and to dissolve.

So, the courage to be, is also the courage to accept that we will dissolve, that we will die.

Even when we know this, we never will know what it is going to be like and what may come up. We are afraid of pain, of a never-ending sickness, of getting dependent or losing our brain function. Fear always shows the worst case! To get old is a process as many others before in our life. A friend of mine said, "Getting old is like the masterpiece of our life!" It is a masterpiece, because it calls forth all our gained wisdom and love for ourselves. It is a special challenge of trust, surrender, and the courage to live through it with a curiosity which sees it as a unique personal experience. We know much about dying, but little about death itself. In most societies we do not have a natural attitude towards death. Letting go is sometimes so hard for the person him/herself and for those being close, touched, and involved.

Gilbert, on the tellers chair, had a very low voice when he started to talk. "I was so happy that my father came with my mother to a meeting with my new partner and her parents. He never visited me before. But I was shaken and it was very difficult for me to see how he decomposes, how tired and depressed he is. It made me sad and somehow helpless. In my inner perception of childhood he was always the one I looked up to, the big one, and I was the small one. This meeting changed a lot. Even I knew in my heart 'you always will stay my father, 'I knew at the same time' I am no more the little one.' My father was an old man, no more enjoying his life, and myself I felt strong and joyful. But still, I felt shaken."

As it often happens in Playback Theatre, Gilbert chose as teller's actor a man, who at that time was busy with the same subject. The story was acted out in three short sequences: as father and child; as a man, tired from all the work (making money, raising children, building a house); and as the man Gilbert is now, ambivalent between helplessness and letting go. Gilbert's last sentence was: "Thank you for everything – but don't go yet!"

The next story in short, told by a woman, picked up the subject in another connection.

"My father died fifteen years ago. I remember him as a very young man and I missed him. Watching Gilbert's story brought back the memory of my father. I didn't get the experience of somebody getting old and had no time to experience this process. I even couldn't talk to him anymore. He just wasn't there anymore and I forgot him. I hear people talking about their parents getting old and what it feels like. I suddenly felt that it is like a piece of life that I missed."

After the "Let's watch," from the conductor, the playing back included the sudden loss and longing of a young girl and also the 'missing piece' of life's experiences. It ended with the question of the teller's actor: "Will I experience getting old?"

If stories of fear (fear of death, of the unknown,) or stories, which seem difficult to tell (because of the intensity or intimacy of feelings) are told in Playback Theatre, we know that there is trust in this theatre, in the compassion of the team and in the audience. It expresses that deeper levels can be touched. To be ready to play back the fear and the truth, we first need to have a look at our own fear, our own deeper subjects, to find the courage and the understanding to play them back authentically. Since we are the mirror, we are accepting what is. This acceptance is our base. The expression of it on stage radiates safety.

"The courage to be" is the willingness to accept ourselves and life – with all the many facets it will bring along.

The citation tells us that it is more important to rely on our authenticity than on false images, because they are trying to shape us into what we are not and we might miss our own life.

The citation also teaches us that there is no other way to deal with pain, fear, and situations which seem unacceptable, than to find the courage to get along with what life presents to us. To be in this present life means always to be in the right place. Here lays the key to an inner peace. Loving self-acceptance has an impact on how I move through life, and also on how we all move through this time of upheaval.

If we want to be somewhere else than where life takes us, we are going to be in a fight.

If we need to be different than we are, it's going to be difficult for us.

If we wish to die in a certain way, we will realize that we have no control over this. Even by committing suicide we don't know what this experience will be like.

We cannot choose our life – we only can live it. Life is not what we expect it to be: it is what we allow it to be. Life is challenging us only as much as it trusts us to be able to manage it. Whatever is happening to us in our life, at the end it is always us, the only possible person, which can be able to live with it, to deal with it, and also the only person who is able to like it.

We can be at peace with everything, if we drop all the judgments about how we should be, about how things should be.

Can we be in peace with our funny personality?

Sometimes we need support to accept life as it is.

Playback Theatre gives this support. We see the actors finding the right expression. We see acceptance by seeing our story played back in a respectful way.

In Playback Theatre we cannot change the story. We cannot take away the pain. We have no control over life. But, we can transfer our empathy for this moment or story told. We can be with the teller in an almost unbearable situation and share the suffering or share an ultimate feeling of joy. What we do is 'only' having the courage to accept a piece of life by bringing it on stage as being true.

That's all we can do. And it is so much!

With the compassion of the team on stage plus the excitement of the audience watching, we can say that the story is 'in good hands.' It belongs to all. It gets incorporated in the community as one part of all the other human experiences, and therefore gets contained in the whole. The 'being included' of a person and the inclusion of the past within stories is a gift to humanity and can change the future. We need courage and openness to accept the importance of integrating the past.

When we pray, we pray not only for money, for a lover, for health, for being a good person and maybe different, but mainly we pray that 'God' looks at us with loving eyes! If we were able to look at ourselves with these loving eyes, we would be better able to accept ourselves. If, as actors, as musician and as conductor, we are able to look at the teller and the audience with those loving eyes, we certainly will be in the right vibe! We accept any personal experience.

We need to be very careful and aware of the way we are looking at ourselves and the way we think about others. Mostly we are very fast with our judgments – and there are many! In Playback Theatre we need to be sensitive of how we tune into what is told to us. Playback Theatre does not perceive people by their shortcomings.

Swiss Cheese ('Emmentaler') has many holes and not much cheese. Our imprint or learning in our western society is to see the shortcomings, that which is not good enough or what is missing. We are constantly judging. We are used to seeing the holes and not the cheese!

There is something happening on Playback Theatre's stage which we can see as a start for just being ourselves. When you tell your story, there is nobody else other than you and your unique story told, with all the different feelings – including the unacceptable ones. And, since your story becomes a real piece of theatre, a piece of art with heart, you might feel that you can be at peace with the story. Being at peace with your story means to bring the story "home." We feel it best in our heart. We stop fighting and by doing so, we value what is happening to us and value our life a little bit more. Evolving our consciousness in Playback Theatre in this way, we also evolve our perception. By relating to others and their lives we surpass the 'I' and can find a 'we' which is much wider and inclusive.

"Theatre of Love" is not a sentimental, soft expression, but describes a theatre that opens our heart to be human.

The facts described above are not always obvious, nor necessarily conscious. There is just a feeling of being contained in a space of being "right." We can see it, for example, in the face of the teller.

Acceptance really is a fine art!

"Holding the sacred space where all stories are welcome, acting upon the very edge of the unknown, is a hard craft as well as simple magic….It is our gift to the world and frees our deepest core," said Veronica Needa, president of the IPTN, in 2001.

A bond exists between "communitas, liminality, and lowermost status." Turner, Dramas, Fields, and Metaphors, 1974

In Playback Theatre the teller's chair is for everybody!

This citation takes us to another subject: We also want and need people from the lowermost status on the tellers chair.

If people should be treated equally – like Playback Theatre does – it certainly would mean some big changes in society.

It definitely would mean 'liminality'!

To understand Turner's expressions we will go on a short detour, to a summary of their definitions:

Communitas: According to Turner, all societies have an idea of society as a social structure (segmented categories of unequal people), which is contrasted with a desire for society to be a homogenous, undifferentiated, authentically whole, and embracing the idea of communitas. Communitas can be thought of as a collective bond that comes at a certain point to connect individuals that before were separate. It happens as a phase in the process of building a community, in which social structures are released or dissolved for people to be equal and connected.

To understand liminality, we can find comprehensive set phrases, such as 'betwixt and between,' 'transitional,' 'becomingness' and 'borderland.' It is a space of uncertainty, which at the same time allows a flexible entryway into a sense of pure essence to get in touch with what we call numinous. So it is in these liminal situations where communitas emerges in the form of spontaneous sociability, love for each other, a sense of solidarity and equality and heightened emotional, cathartic or spiritual experience. Liminal is usually associated with a sense that people have removed the masks of the ordinary social world; people involved have become genuine, authentic individuals, free of the restraints of social obligations. Status loses its normal importance. In the state of liminality, we not only get shaken, but also those who have been at the bottom of the system become intermingled. While in the liminal state, human beings are stripped of anything that might differentiate them from their fellow human beings – they are in between the social structure, "temporarily fallen through the cracks, so to speak, and it is in these cracks, in the interstices of social structure, that they are most aware of themselves. Yet liminality is a midpoint between a starting point and an ending point, and as such it is a temporary state that ends when we find ourselves back, reincorporated into a social structure."

The following example is my own experience with liminality:

Moving from Europe to Asia seriously brought me into an 'in-betwixt and in-between' state. Every time I travel from Indonesia (where I live now) back to Europe, I have a hard time and it is always like a culture-shock seeing people rushing, buying, having no time, being so busy. It is also difficult at first to join the subjects they are talking about. Their need to function in a system is huge. As result, there is stress and anxiety. Often I can feel suffering, even though they are well fed and live in nice places.

When there is silence for a while and when we can relax and share what really happened to us, it usually releases my feeling of nearly being a stranger and 'not to belong there anymore.' But, coming back from Europe to Bali is also difficult! I never will belong here. My woven pattern is so different. Balinese are just knitted differently! It is the island of the 'Gods and Demons.' It is hard for Western people to understand their life, because they live with all those invisible worlds in their daily life, their actions and thinking. The hidden social and also religious rules are hard to capture. There is always friendliness and always a smile, but also something unpredictable and astonishing, because you can't figure out the behind. No Balinese ever wants to 'lose his face!' To have a friend is something different for them than for me. For me it is deep talks and sharing, while for them it just amounts to social contact. Balinese don't talk about their feelings and hardly at all about personal matters. When I meet 'a friend,' I want to hug her/him. But they don't hug. I never saw a man hugging his wife in all these years.

Bali is so different than all the other countries I got to know. My way to live life seemed strange and my way to relate was also strange for them. Something was difficult for me. It felt like a tightrope walk: Where do I need to adapt and where are the limits, so I still can be myself and it feels good?

To be too long in liminality is not healthy – it makes us crazy! I knew, liminal must be a phase and not a state of being. The more I understood about the Balinese way of thinking, about the background of their social life and their thousands of different ceremonies, the more I could accept my own limits and my own valuable way to go through life. I was able to surf between the two worlds, to join in and to keep out. I am 'stable' now, and at the same time enriched. And I am not frustrated anymore, when for example children run crying to their mothers, because I am the first white person they have ever seen and they think that I am a demon!

The only man in our small Playback Theatre company is called Nyoman. He is Balinese and also got into liminality. Two years ago he colored a stripe of his hair in the middle of his head. He explained that he has a split head and always has strong headaches. The main reasons, he found out, were those different worlds he experienced playing with us.

"Sometimes, I am so confused with my and all your other thinking," Nyoman told us. "But, I am so happy Playback Theatre is in my life. I learn so much about life!"

The examples above touch in many ways the problems concerning the immigration of people from other countries into 'our' country.

They also show how Playback Theatre can bridge diversities and ease this process. In the liminal we not only get troubled and shaken, but we get a chance for transformation and can come back with a treasure, a new knowledge and perception. In Playback Theatre we can meet on a common level where our diversities lose their importance, because here we are touched by stories and our humanness. We get a feeling of a 'universal' connection. We make an evolutionary step.

This is an important part of Playback Theatre's contribution to social change.

On stage we often experience liminality. As playbackers, we find ourselves, in fact, most of the time in liminality. We are no longer totally ourselves and never totally the other person.

Playback Theatre surpasses social status. We address each other with our first names. We don't know if the person next to us is a dishwasher or a bank director.

We watch the puzzle of people in a performance and encourage those who never speak up. We try to reach those of the lowermost status in many ways. For example, there are companies who go to prisons and play back the stories of the prisoners. The teller's chair is for everybody!

In the normal outside world the rules are different than in Playback Theatre. Here there is a different atmosphere. It is here, where change can happen.

The ritual of Playback Theatre allows entrance into a space of "becoming." The intensity varies depending on the setting, situation and other factors within a performance. Personal stories are the bridge to intimacy. This is the shift to other levels. Maybe we get a little shaken when we experience passing the borders of our normal judgments and perception. But, in this space we can be touched by something unspeakable. Our heart center spreads out. We start seeing people from a different angle. We see them more from the inside. Slowly we take off our daily masks. We find human beings who are individuals, and unique. At the same time the diversity of stories enlarges, and we get closer. We realize that we all have a worthwhile story. We can be authentic and lose our shyness about being truthful. We are aware and feel consciously that something special is happening in the here and now.

The concept of Playback Theatre leads into a process that unfolds naturally. The outcome is to get a feeling for an essential bond uniting us and slowly transcending superficial differences, passing through liminality towards community.

Since liminality is a temporary state, and since the ritual of a Playback Theatre performance has a clear beginning and a clear ending, we won't get lost. But, we find ourselves enriched, open and more connected back in normal life, in the known structure.

We easily can understand now that "a bond exists between liminality, communitas and the lowermost status."

In Playback Theatre all is happening in such a short time, and often with lasting impression. Something keeps staying in our memory.

The first quote with its citations are the first steps of our stairs.

The main value lays in our basic attitude towards every story and every human being.

We have been looking at the first quote quite elaborately, because we see it as the basis for all further ones.

AS A COMMUNITY WE ARE WISE

In Western societies we are conditioned to think as 'I.' As more 'I,' or 'me,' is put in the foreground, the more egocentric the culture will become. But, if there is no 'I,' but only the 'we,' as in some cultures, we will find people in a totally different field of frequencies. This 'we' might miss some of the importance of the individual. Without the individual's consciousness of the importance of the 'I,' we may miss an important step towards a 'we,' which makes a community strong, because it's carried by each single member.

Playback Theatre has its focus on the 'we,' on community and on connection, but by first looking at the individual. Taking individual stories as the vehicle for coming together, for finding a common ground of being human, is a gentle, true action towards a wider field of deepened human relations and, therefore, a possibility of peace.

Our small planet, called Earth, is one of an untold number of other planets with their stars and suns, located at the edge of the Milky Way.

In the universe everything is completely interactive and interdependent. Energetically seen, there is only one life and one consciousness – the origin of all and everything – an endless mystery!

In this energy-field, everything is basically in its right place and movement. Information is transmitted by energies in a speed we cannot imagine.

Since man is the microcosm of the macrocosm, we are only one design of a much larger complexity. We are embedded in this energy field. It's amazing to imagine that nobody can fall out of the universe. We never can get lost!

Only, on the level of life on this planet, we still have the feeling of being separate. Our sense of separateness has diverse and complex reasons. To put it simply, it is the separative quality of the mind.

The outcome is that we never stand together and by that we support indirectly what grieves us the most.

Therefore, our next step of building our stairs is finding togetherness, finding the 'we.'

Let's have a look at the word 'wise.' The word 'wise' is related to life, to experiences in and about our personal and interactive lives.

In German there is a saying: "Who knows others is clever; who knows him/her-self is wise."

This means that to know myself includes an understanding of what it means to be human. It means that I am deeply connected to myself and to life. As a wise person, I know about life's cycles and movements and about its ending and death. I know about my value and also about my limitations. I contribute to the world in my special way, but I am not forcing or pressuring myself towards or into something which is out of reach.

To be in connection with oneself helps us to be more clear and calm. We don't need to fight to be right. There is less pressure and more openness.

In a wise community, we see the importance of our interactions.

In a community where we can connect and share, a wider field of experiencing life opens up. We enlarge our emotional and intellectual spectrum by insights and understanding. We expand our limited sight. We are aware of our diversities and similarities. If we are conscious of the beauty of our (warm) connectedness, we can develop a new sense of commonness and see the importance and the gain of collaborating. The individual is protected and supported by a wise community.

As a wise community we always have in mind that we are part of a much wider spectrum or complexity, and therefore we are wise enough to be aware that wisdom is not something that can just be accumulated. Wisdom is always there and we just have to open up to it. Wisdom lies in the intricate web of relationship with ourselves, with each other, and with the wider world. By trusting and opening up all our senses, we connect with this web and tap into its wisdom.

The second quote, being focused on the 'we,' takes us to the importance of relating and connecting as the basis for a community. Discrimination and differentiation in our thinking are needed to find the values which integrate all.

Playback Theatre's concept is offering us a wonderful chance to transfer our knowledge, gained by listening and playing back, directly into the community.

Therefore, we walk on to the first citation:

"Knowledge is not extended from those who consider they know to those who consider that they do not know. Knowledge is built up in relations between human beings and the world."
Freire, Education for Critical Consciousness, 1973

In Playback Theatre we are learning not only to understand and acknowledge each individual's specific relationship to life, but also the importance of becoming a real community.

Every story told is about relating, about the relation to ourselves, to others, to life and to the world. Relating is the core of life's dynamics.

All aspects concerning human relations are contained in stories: the joy, the suffering and pain, the conflicts, the enlightenment, the normal, the sadness, the fear – all those 'delicious' experiences we have looked at in the first quote.

With every story told and played back on Playback Theatre's stage, we can learn about the dynamics, the variety and diversity of relating. We see the reality of all kind of different relations and therefore we need to take care of them in an appropriate way. For this we need knowledge.

On stage we want to make the narrative transparent, visible and understandable, so people can experience and share their stories. We don't hide truth – we want to be the witness of the truth.

In Playback Theatre we ask for personal experiences. This is delicate, because there is this special moment of silence: the wish to stay hidden and the irresistible longing to tell.

Playing back a story or moment means to get in a personal relationship with the teller. This act of relating will bring an echo. It triggers the yearning in people to unveil their own story.

By exploring different characters in our rehearsals and our playing back, by role-reversal with almost everything (objects, symbols, animals or nature), we gain our needed knowledge. By exchanging ideas and by getting more conscious about our judging mind, we get more critical about our assumptions and conditioned beliefs. In our joint actions we gain such a lot of insight and it is seems that our knowledge is perfecting itself!

Experiencing the world and the life of human beings in this way takes us to another level where we can find new meaning.

The primary motivating force in man is striving to find a purpose and a meaning in one's life. Meaning is one's personal dedication to a cause greater then oneself. We seek an answer for the 'why' for living, for getting up every morning.

In Playback Theatre we can discover a kind of meaning, which gives reason and passion for life.

"Through Playback Theatre we can find reflections that can bring meaning to us and our world. We, as human beings, need stories for our emotional health and our sense of purposeful existence. In this sense, Playback Theatre can contribute to the universal quest for meaning." (J. Fox)

Meaning is always the result of an internal process. This process underlies a higher order, which certainly could be explained by neuropsychology. We are not going on this detour. It is like something within us is selecting and collecting things and throwing them up to see if they fit somewhere. When something fits, we discovered a new meaning. It is like saying, "Aha!"

Meaning can flow between or among us when we listen and respond to each other. This happens on different levels in Playback Theatre. It is amazing and beautiful when we are watching and being aware of the developing connections in the audience. They are not taking place by talking, but by an unspoken language. Hearts are getting connected by shared narratives, by the actions on stage and by the flow of emotions and thoughts.

We can gain knowledge by loosening up some of the rules we all have been taught to live by. Without being totally aware, we connect to strangers or to people who look different, dress differently, have a different way to express themselves, or walk in different steps through life.

The richness and effectiveness of this theatre comes from allowing all dimensions to be there, echoing and illuminating each other. All can benefit from this process.

We are joining other lives and, without noticing, we surpass status, cultures, borders and religions.

How much information and energy is gently moved in Playback Theatre through our hearts and consciousness! A web, out of many strings, gets woven.

Stories have a transmitter function between humans.

A story filled with emotional energy is transported from one human being to many. A story can pick up several different waves out of our life that carry on within us. Stories and moments are not only told – they are played back and, by this, the story is put in a new and energetically heightened state. This multiplies and intensifies the transmitter function.

I had left my Playback Theatre company in Switzerland after thirteen years for love and marriage in New Mexico, and I went to one of their performances. Of course I was very excited and also wanted to tell a story. I had one in mind, which seemed so important to share. I never told it! I got caught by a different theme in a story of another woman, raised my hand and suddenly sat on the teller's chair, telling an old, nearly forgotten story about my brother, with whom I never found a deep connection. In the play back it touched me strongly to see my endless efforts to reach him. Watching this on stage, I immediately got an new impulse: "Don't force it. Stop trying – just wait!" That was so releasing.

The energies of the former stories transported me to a subject which was beyond the story I was thinking of before.

The images of a story of somebody else can stay in our memory for quite a while. They may bother us consciously. We need to think about them, or they may pop up suddenly in our life.

Other people also get touched by our stories. In other words, stories are "woken up."

When we try to look at the process and at the stories following each other, it is always cryptic why and what is picked up during a performance. How often we wonder about it. In some way we will never be able to really explain it. We can watch something which we call "the red thread in Playback Theatre." We can have a glance into the mystery of life and a feeling of our deeper links.

The unconscious is wise – it is connected to life.

Life strives for movement, sometimes stirs up and shakes rigid forms, balances out disharmony, strives for completion and never leaves one part behind.

The next story will balance out the painful one before. Becoming aware of the invisible energy flow, the unseen and unconscious connections among us, we will learn that, especially in Playback Theatre, there is a deeper flow beyond which we can trust.

In one of our performances I really started to get nervous, because after playing back some different moments, the pairs told were quite heavy inner conflicts and the following two stories were unpleasant and sad experiences. At this moment – as a conductor – I was trying to think of something which could shift gears. I was afraid that the performance would only consist of life's difficult side. But before I had the time to think of an image to gently move the wave towards more calm waters, the next teller raised her hand.

Jane sat on the teller's chair. After a deep breath, she said, "Yesterday was my birthday and I decided, unlike of all the years before, to stay alone. Before, I always made a lovely party for all my friends. But this year, not. I didn't want to carry all those bottles and all the nice food up to the third floor – I wanted just to celebrate myself. I got a tasty pizza from the Italian shop, lit a candle, and listened to my favorite music. Later I sat there quietly by the open window. The music had finished. Suddenly I heard some noise and I was a little anxious – but it was only a cat which appeared in the window. It was one of the neighbor's cats. After a while she came inside and laid beside me on the floor. I like to sit on the floor. There was only silence – silence supported by the noises from the road down below. I was alone and not alone. The cat was here, but I was just being with myself, maybe for the first time. It was awesome......I cannot describe it, but I felt a new kind of happiness....mhhh.... I still can feel it now."

The actors, except the teller's actor and the cat, created with the musician a touching chorus with movement and colored cloths, which ended in silent movements.

For me, this was an amazing learning experience; I learned to trust the "red thread!" I learned to trust the unconscious and to believe in the life-force beyond all. I no longer get nervous from two or more threatening stories. I just know now: I can trust. This raises my heartbeat, at the same time turning it into a peaceful vibe.

In Playback Theatre we find a community of fellowship.

On stage we learn to trust. We experience that we can rely on each other. Our play back is a joint action. It is the challenge of a real team-work. We are servants for one another. We are servants for the teller and the audience.

"Serving is somehow like communion: communion is more than anything else a gift. In giving, we are given too and we end up with riches of the sort which fills the pockets of the soul." (J. Fox)

We experience that serving in this way is nourishing. It is food for our heart, soul and spirit.

For many of us this is a new insight: it transforms the notion that service, for example, belongs to those of lowermost status or to some cultural images of women.

Playback Theatre means serving; it means surfing on different levels of life and experiencing various dimensions.

These are, in fact, life-teachings for everybody.

We learn through stories of others. There is a kernel of wisdom in each narrative. We learn about life. Playback Theatre is the only theatre which directly offers a practicing ground for life.

From there, wisdom arises.

We gain our knowledge through interaction and our shared experiences.

"I suggest that the movement towards coherence is innate, but our thought has muddled it." Bohm, On Dialogue, 1996

There is a natural tendency for water to flow towards the sea.

There is also a natural tendency of meaning to flow towards a state of coherence.

Without development of the mind we wouldn't have the consciousness of relationships with others and know that we are alive!

What causes separation is that we are caught in our thinking.

The mind thinks it must rule and be in control of our life. But, here we have a problem: most of our thoughts are collective thoughts, inherited from the collective conscious, but not our own. The society which put them out is "incoherent," which means in some way unbalanced and not clearly focused. For this reason, also, our actions with one another are out of step and incoherent.

For centuries we have lived a mind-dominated life. But, the role of the mind has to shift, because our consciousness and awareness has emerged as something much more differentiated. We are ready now to think on our own!

The doorway to transformation is engaging the mind. The mind must learn what to watch, which also means differentiation.

In Playback Theatre we can contemplate and discover life's different possibilities. We meet to explore and share our experiences of being human and to find the lost coherence by the intimacy on our stage. The mind's original creativity and its nature of inspiration could contribute to the quality of life on our planet.

We can use the mind as tool for observation, discrimination and reflection – a playground of joy, and as a friend!

Our exercises often are focused on awareness, on the "beyond," on our sensitivity for the body and our thoughts, on the energy between us, on our personal feelings and spontaneous reactions, on our intuition, and more. In this way, we can discover a new point of view and other qualities of our mind.

This theatre "reaches down to the deep, undying need for connection, to be worthwhile, to be heard, to be affirmed and welcomed as one who shares the human condition. We can get connected by emotions and life currents far deeper than the specific details of our individual experience. Through the stories of others, we can see our own life. Behind each individual story there is an expanded one which transcends it." (J. Fox)

Without commonness we cannot survive long on this small planet – this is an illusion of our thinking. Playback Theatre opens a door to lead us gently back to the original movement. Sharing our personal lives by stories and moments and experiencing coherence as the outcome of Playback Theatre's concept of playing back, we slowly realize that a shift takes place, which turns the longing into something basic and normal.

This is the beauty of Playback Theatre: we are able to put new values to our thinking, our mind and our heart.

The human mind is like a fertile ground where seeds are continually being planted. The seeds are mostly opinions, ideas and concepts, which too often have been linked with fear. That's how the mind got fertile for the seeds of fear. Every human mind is fertile, but only for those kinds of seeds it is prepared for. We can prepare it to receive the seeds of trust, so that feelings of commonness can grow.

In Playback Theatre we can plant those seeds.

Seen from this perspective, Playback Theatre is also operating as a fertilizer!

We already can see the plants growing. They still need to be taken care of to get strong. This process, within ourselves and within the world, takes time.

"Communities...have a history—in an important sense they are constituted by their past—and for this reason we can speak of a real community as a 'community of memory,' one that does not forget its past. In order not to forget that past, a community is involved in retelling its story, its constitutive narrative, and in so doing, it offers examples..."
Bellah et al., Habits of the Heart, 1985

Couples like to tell how and where they have met and (mostly) their eyes start shining. The memory brings back the original connection.

This is also true for communities. Mostly it is a vision, full of energy and hope, which is the source of finding togetherness as a community. Playback Theatre was created out of a vision for the good of all and the world. To look at our history as a Playback Theatre community means to remember how we came together, why we joined, and what makes Playback Theatre so precious.

Not to forget the past means not to forget the kernel of where we came from, to keep the original vision in mind and to take the past as a reminder to stay on the right track. It's in the past where the fire got started and from where we take the flame for the future. This flame is the focus of the community and without it, it will fall apart.

If we change the focus we are in danger of losing the original value. If we change the meaning we must consequently change the name so it will fit the new form or agenda.

To look at the "Quotes on Basic Values of Playback Theatre" means to look at its constitution and original vision. We are reminded of its genius basics, we see better its gift and our responsibility within.

Sometimes, we are tempted to forget about the origin of our enthusiasm for acting, inventing and experiencing. Sidetracks are important, but to not lose the main track is of basic importance. For this, our exchange and sharing, our understanding of "where we are coming from and where we are going," is a necessity. Playback Theatre never can be just entertainment. Stories of people are not toys – they are our joys!

The basic value of Playback Theatre is about opening up to a wider view of the whole world and the people within it. We see the importance of a community, because it is more than the sum of the single parts. We realize that knowledge comes out of experiences. Playback Theatre is not only taking care of the individual, but also seeing the preciousness and creating chances for togetherness. Our longing for connection finds fulfillment in Playback Theatre.

We already are a wise community, still challenged in our seriousness, challenged to accept the conditions set by those who teach us wisely, challenged to put our wholeheartedness on top of rigid training curricula, and challenged to find the right balance between reasonable structure and flexibility.

Our challenge is also to find the beauty and joy in our task of bringing Playback Theatre as a "gift of value" in a meaningful way to all people of every status and culture. The beauty lays in the discovery of the variety of human beings on Earth, and in finding connection.

Our walk has led us to the value of being together. We found the reasons of the why, and of the how.

EVERYONE IS A (CREATIVE) ACTOR

Many people say that they cannot act.

But, on Playback Theatre's stage they can.

Why? Playback Theatre is mainly a theatre of the heart.

At our wedding party (as well as at our divorce party!), we put in-between other activities (like some speeches, songs or sketches, and a menu split into five parts), rather short sequences of Playback Theatre. There were moments or stories told about love, relations and life. Friends without knowledge and practice in Playback Theatre were acting, and they did wonderfully.

If, in our Playback Theatre company Schaffhausen in Switzerland, we were only a few actors at a performance or in other special situations, we invited people from the audience to come up on stage to act with us. Often it was surprising and also hilarious how they filled in a role.

If we are carried through the action by the others, if we capture the main idea and don't need to be "a star," we can be an actor on Playback Theatre's stage.

Everyone can be an actor according the third quote.

We are all actors in our life and play different roles during this life. We play them in varying perfection or imperfection. Some seem not to fit in our repertoire. Some don't go easily together, and we feel the conflicts or ambivalence of competing roles that can give us a hard time. Some we play perfectly – some too perfectly! – and some we don't know yet about.

When we think of a creative person, we find words like: imaginative, ingenious, innovative, inventive and original.

Creativity has to do with ideas, imagination, inspiration, sudden insights, intuition, illumination and associations; with touching the consciousness of the universe, letting the unconscious speak, and being in contact with the creative spirit.

Creativity can show up in so many different forms. It could show up when we invent a new recipe, by exploring a new way of doing things, or if we follow an impulse to bring a small dream into reality. Often, there are special feelings coming along with it – we wonder how we did it, and we are happy about our ideas.

Concerning Playback Theatre, the third quote will lead us to another level of our potential. In the core of each one of us we find this "God-like" source: creativity! Creativity is a layer beyond all. It is like bringing beauty on stage with colors and sparks, which even make unique sounds.

To be creative, we must lose our fear of being wrong.

Staying on our walk, we are going to explore art in Playback Theatre.

"Art is immanent to all men, and not only to a select few; art is not to be sold, no more than are breathing, thinking, loving. Art is not merchandise." Boal, Theatre of the Oppressed, 1979

Many artists struggle over this first citation.

But, the desire to create, to make something, to express ourselves is imminent in human beings. The real meaning of art in Playback Theatre and the reason why it is described as a basic value, lies on a different level than seen from a materialistic point of view. It has nothing to do with money, or with success.

Art in Playback Theatre has something to do with aesthetics and originality. It is about intensifying the energy on stage. It increases the level of participation.

Art is fulfilling, exciting and makes us vibrate in a special way.

Art on stage is touching our eyes. We see beauty on stage. We see the actors changing miraculously into 'real' other persons. We see different relationships, landscapes and insides of houses. Music in Playback Theatre is art. Art is touching our ears. We hear sounds of a music which is fitting the actions on stage, as if they were made as one. We hear the sounds of feelings, moods and dreams. Art is touching our heart. We can become one with the teller or with other figures and we can experience the many feelings contained in all those different stories, portrayed with compassion. The outcome is the so-called "awe."

Even art in our acting is one of many aspects to be considered within our trainings; it is the one aspect which transcends our actions. It connects us to that so-called 'divine' space of colors, sparks and falling stars, which is creativity. Seen from this level, we could say that art and creativity can lift a 'drama' or scene on stage to a condensation of truth and beauty, an actor into some kind of a magical being, or a team into an image of a being which is conducted by an invisible guide.

To be a creative actor means risk-taking, to be open to being touched from inside by some layers beyond and bringing our creativity and spontaneity on stage into the play of all.

Art in Playback Theatre is surprise!

Art in Playback Theatre means translation.

We are nothing more, nothing less than translators.

Translators listen carefully and speak many languages!

We need to listen, to understand and to feel what we heard – this is the foundation of art in Playback Theatre. Second, we want to translate it. We find expressions with the body, with our mime, combined with words or sounds. We translate it to other levels, connect it to images, fantasy, symbols and metaphors. We translate energies into space and voice, emotions into movement.

To be a translating actor means to be real, to know what we are doing and how we can present our role in its fullest expression. At the same time we don't know anything.

We are open and prepared for that part of our creativity which is inspiration and intuition and comes to us from a mysterious source. We experience it as flashing sparks, not knowing where it came from, but seeing it as a gift. We also could say: "God kissed us!"

This kiss translated into our action is seen and felt by the other actors. Since we are dependent on our teamwork, each 'kiss' will not only be supported by the others, but it also inspires them.

Our mind, heart and body is translating the story into another language without changing the reality. We bring it into space, enlarge or reduce parts. We make 'real' what has been invisible. It means to only touch some of the reality to bring out the teller's truth. It is surpassing the frame of time. We use speed and slow motion to intensify some parts. We all try to reach beyond! In this moment our acting is a joint translation.

If we translate the story or the moment told in this way, then it will be real art. It will be a surprise: deep, spontaneous, meaningful, touching and simply true.

Beauty and art have to do with transcendence, with a connection to our spirit, where we get in touch with a deeper knowledge or with the "Unseen." We are touched by or get in touch with our creativity, with the kernel of ideas and images. We pick it up (or we get picked up by it) and quickly it grows from a seed into a flower, popping up on stage. And later, after flourishing, it disappears again.

Creative actions make us feel alive and bring us together. We are delighted! We also feel the healing potential of our play and of our playing back.

To express and play back what we as a team have heard and to be the translators we would like to be, calls for regular trainings. In the intimate space of our rehearsals we open up to many different subjects: the ability to relate and to cooperate with one another, our willingness to experience liminality, to trust and to believe in our spontaneity and creativity. We think less, and at the same time we develop the awareness of never losing touch with our focus: We play back a story, a personal experience of a human being present within the audience or the group.

Now we come to the question: How do we become an authentic actor?

C.G. Jung talks about a "well-fitting persona," like a well-fitting mask. It means that what we show to the outside in our behavior and in our actions should be in tune with our inside world and the different parts within us. With a well-fitting persona we are flexible, creative and highly authentic. We are real and others perceive us as trustworthy. But as we have seen in quote one, our 'persona' is not always in tune with our inside world.

The completed form (or the form of completion)

A plant or a flower cannot be anything other than a completion. Have you ever seen an ugly flower? The flower unfolds depending on its inner design.

Sometimes the plant has to adapt to the environment it is growing in. Since it wants to survive and to reach its highest potential, it may have to make some changes in its growth.

I like this image and I like to transfer it to humans, because basically every human being also has this kind of an inner design. We also want to find our form of completion or the uniqueness of the being we are meant to be. But as the plants, we get shaped, cut and twisted, and hardly grow according to our innate kernel. Also our outer form is often not appropriate to what we really are.

Sometimes the seed is not even visible, but the inner seed is still there, hidden underneath, hoping to be discovered, sometimes popping up.

If an inner form (our inner being) is contained in the outer form (our appearance and expression) and is accurate to the world, we can talk of a completed form.

This would be in Jungian terminology the "well-fitting persona."

A completed form in Playback Theatre would mean that each role is in accordance with ourselves, the teller, the story and the audience. My acting as the teller's actor is a true role reversal and a clear mirror. My authentic acting as actor is representing the inner and outer situation of the role I have been chosen for, and is a congruent part within the dynamics of the whole story. As musician the completed form means that our music is linking everything. It is connecting and structuring the inside and the outside with sound. As conductor my completed form is multifaceted and in congruence with the needs of the audience, the actors and the teller.

Isn't the inner situation, acted out in an appropriate way, what we want to see as teller – the kernel of truth acted out as a piece of art? As actors we try to catch our important part in the story, to fill the role as best we can to make the story as visible and deep as it is.

"Acts of Service" is the title of Jonathan Fox's book.

As actors on stage, we show the reality of the flower and its experience; we nourish the roots and we convey acceptance. We serve the flower. By serving one flower, we also serve the other flowers a little bit.

We are striving for the right tune, the adequacy of the story and for the truth of its content. By this, the flower begins to unfold.

This is more than watching your story, and it's more than playing back somebody's story.

The completed form of a story played back means that the outer form, the story itself, must contain the inner world of the teller.

The whole story has an inner form, which we call the essence. The outer form is a composition, built up by the actors in cooperation to make the inner form visible. The more congruent outer and inner form are, the more 'completed' is the playback.

Each actor has to reduce his outer form according to the inner form of the story. By this, also, the inner form of the story gets reduced to its essence.

The kind of art which is evolving out of this process and out of our cooperation will have a special beauty and truth.

In our playing back, we must be true. We cannot fake. We do not want to fake. We cannot cheat by playing just anything.

This kind of art truly cannot be sold.

The completed form doesn't mean that nothing can be added anymore, only that nothing can be taken away anymore. What a difference! The greatest accomplishment lies in its simplicity.

There is another aspect of our subject completion: male and female.

We will only touch this fascinating subject shortly. Not only in life, but also in Playback Theatre, male and female energy should be balanced. They are highly dependent on each other to create harmony. Completion comes out of a process of the male and female energy working together. In fact, it is like a dance. Playback Theatre's ritual has a balance between male and female.

The structure of Playback Theatre has a clear form which is more male, or father-like. Our playing back and the dialogue with people is more female, or mother-like.

The male energy sets the ritual and frame like a container – for the female energy to bring in it's creativity. By their cooperation and inter-dependency, they can reach harmony and their highest potential. To integrate the idea of the female and male concept in our playback trainings, we might have a look at our own male and female sides, to unveil the mysteries of the female, and to go on a quest for maleness. We will gain an understanding of their archetypal base and their energies. We can transfer these energies into our play, no matter if we are a man or a woman.

Art in Playback Theatre is the outcome of a process which reduces outside matters to its inside essence.

Essence means that we reach beyond reality to express the imagination which created it! Finding the essence of a story from a non-judgmental and 'authentic' place depends on our ability to physically convey information and feeling.

Our rehearsals are filled with exercises to increase our skills and to become a creative actor.

"Place this three-year-old in a room with other threes and sooner or later they will become an acting company."
Paley, Mollie is Three: Growing Up in School, 1986.

Paley's citation brings us to subjects which concern our playfulness, spontaneity and cooperation. In Playback Theatre we need to discover and to reconnect to the playful child. Creativity is like a pond, a basic source beyond – as we have seen before.

Mostly, our connection to this pond takes root in childhood.

For the child, life is a creative adventure.

The most basic explorations of a child's world are creative exercises. They have a desire and drive to explore, to find out about things, to try things out, to experiment with different ways of handling things and looking at things. In fact, they begin a lifelong process of inventing themselves. We could even say that in some way every child 'reinvents' language, walking and love. They are like creators of their life. They genuinely have a creative imagination.

Children invent entire universes of reality in their play. They spontaneously play with each other, play freely and without thinking, and get deeply involved in what they are doing. Their world of playing is full of fantasy and doesn't need anything. This doesn't exclude arguing, but as long as grown ups don't interfere, they mostly are able to solve a problem. Children learn about social life and life itself by role-playing. They just cooperate.

Unconsciously, they experience different feelings and different qualities in different roles. It is learning by doing.

Going on a short detour, we will touch another interesting aspect:

In the American Indian tradition of the 'Deer Tribe,' there is a difference between the 'inner child' and the 'spirit child.' One part of the inner child is the hurt child, already cut and twisted, inhibited and ashamed. It is mostly the origin of any creative block. The other part of the inner child is still full of joy, dreams and fantasies. Yet, since it is not totally free, it needs to be nourished and listened to. It needs to be taken care of by our grown-up part.

The 'spirit child' could be called 'the pure us,' that part within us which can never ever get hurt or lost. It is always connected to 'the source and the infinite' and has its basis in trust. We all have this spirit child within us!

In any small child's eyes we still can see that connection. A child is born with this trust.

Since Playback Theatre is an improvisational theatre, playfulness and creativity are basic; we need the playful child! Spontaneity and the ability to play together are basic. In our rehearsals we play all those silly games, giggle and experience nonsense and the scope of imagination. We forget that we are these serious grownups. Games and exercises help us to act more on the spur-of-the-moment or on impulse, more off-the cuff and more spontaneous. We find unknown possibilities in our rehearsals. Creativity and spontaneity are the two pillars and key concepts of Playback Theatre.

"Spontaneity means mind and heart and body surpassing the boundaries of each. Spontaneity means unifying oppositions. Spontaneity is play, is striving, is leaping beyond." (J. Fox)

In our trainings we want to overcome our inhibitory mind, to go beyond interpretation, and to be without shame. Spontaneous play needs courage! We partly want to heal and to free the inner child. We start jumping over our limits. We feel the longing to recover the trust we had in childhood – the trust in life. How many times have we lost it and nearly given up? It is shining through the lines in many stories, including our own stories, which are part of the personal content of our rehearsals.

We are searching for the internal interaction of the grownup and the child.

In Playback Theatre we are always confronted with our imperfection. We never can be perfect, because we are human and have our own history. We don't need to be perfect. We learn to cooperate and to trust in our teamwork. We know that imperfections can be balanced out!

With all our exercises we want to play ourselves free, to find multiple ways of connecting, and to support each other. Our trainings are about serious matters, which we explore with so much fun, laughter and tears.

This is how we enrich ourselves to enrich others!

We even start smiling about ourselves. Sometimes we develop that kind of humor, which can see the truth, the blocks and our twisted parts with a loving smile. The laughter coming out of this kind of humor is the free laughter of a child combined with the wisdom of the adult.

To apply our playfulness with its many facets is the basis for all our actions on stage.

Boal writes about practicing "simultaneous dramaturgy," active involvement of the audience during course of play.
Boal, Theatre of the Oppressed, 1979

The whole process of Playback Theatre is based on the idea of exchange, where an invisible net gets woven on many levels. Playback Theatre is a dynamic building of relationships between many people, and each one of those people is a complex, living system.

"Without you, telling your personal moments and stories, we have nothing to play back. Without audience – no Playback Theatre!" I often said this at the beginning of a performance. Everybody is asked to take part and everyone can contribute. People have heard and now know that we want to hear their stories, to listen to them and to play them back. The conductor, as facilitator and trustworthy guide, encourages (and challenges) the audience to give voice to daily or innermost feelings or experiences from their lives. And suddenly something comes to their lips and wants to get out. They raise their hand or walk forward to the teller's chair.

The 'dramas' coming out of the audience will get condensed on stage. During the playback, when the dramas become visible, there is an echo in the audience. It happens inside people sitting and watching. They are involved, even never saying one word.

In Playback Theatre many things happen simultaneously. Energy flows in all directions between the audience and the team on stage, among the people in the audience and within the team itself. Everybody is somehow energized and woken up in the whole process. The exchange of energy during a performance puts everyone in a heightened state. We don't necessarily see it, but it can be felt. There is a net growing, threads are linked between people, nonverbal connections take place. The music flows to the heart of people and connects them. Even those who cannot tune in well cannot totally disregard the connection.

The world's 'big drama' is shown in the 'small dramas' on stage. Curiosity comes forward, memories and associations are activated, judging inner voices are hushed. We get touched by the intimacy of this theatre and by the openness of others.

In the 'simultaneous dramaturgy' within this process, a shift in our conscious and unconscious perception is taking place and throws us out of our often 'lazy' way of drifting through life.

"The audience theatre is a community theatre. It is the community from which the dramas spring and the actors producing them, and again it is not any community, a community in abstract, but our village and neighborhood, the house in which we live. The actors are not any people, people in abstract, but our people, our fathers and mothers, our brothers and sisters, our friends and neighbors." Moreno, Theater of Spontaneity, 1947

A seed for the idea of Playback Theatre was put in Jonathan's head and heart in a small village during his stay in Nepal, when the people from the village enacted their experiences to one another. It touched him! He saw how it changed their social life and the connections among them.

What Moreno's "Theater of Spontaneity" and Playback Theatre have in common is that both are a theatre for the community. An interactive circle is happening, which is bringing a new spark into people's lives.

After one performance, meeting for a short drink with the audience, a woman came to me and said, "It's the third time I have come to Playback Theatre. Lately I have seen this man who was in the first performance – the one who was telling the story with his son..... you remember?..... and he was looking at a shop window with football stuff. I felt so close to him. It was like he would be a good friend of mine, even though I never have spoken one word with him. I knew that he had changed his mind about his son and wanted to buy a football for him. It touched me deeply. I guess this is what makes Playback Theatre so warm. We get like relatives."

"Yes," I said, "I feel the same…. Jonathan Fox talks about a theatre of neighbors and not of strangers."

In an open Playback Theatre performance, at first we might be strangers – but at the end we are for a moment a newly born community. We seem to know each other; we get linked to strangers. The gap between people gets smaller.

The bridges between people are their stories and our playing back. Through the concept of playing back, stories are also the connection to the collective or to other dimensions and levels. We form connections with other levels and many known and new subjects.

Narratives in Playback Theatre are steps to lose our shyness and to feel connection. They are also steps to experience being worthy or to realize that we are a valuable member of the community. We could also say that they all are steps towards peace. We become more at peace with ourselves and, by becoming more accepting of others, we have less need to fight them.

When I was living part-time in Brazil, friends from different countries and some fellows I didn't know so well were visiting. The composition of people was so diverse that there was a lot of tension. We all felt it. Most of us were not really familiar with Playback Theatre, but I wanted to give it a try and share the gift of 'the gold.' Finally, we agreed to meet each morning and evening for about thirty minutes with the focus to share how each one of us felt at this moment of the day – and to play it back. It was no artistic playing back, but we played back. The result was surprising! The hidden connection, beyond our diversities, growing by our effort of being true and honest, brought some small fruits in form of respect and understanding. We didn't become a harmonious group, but we developed into a bunch of people who could tolerate the existing diversity and tension. This extraordinary experience made me happy, because I saw that acceptance, generated by our way of playing back, presents the possibility of living together without severe fights. I realized that the potential of Playback Theatre is an avenue for peace and that the background of community theatre is "a concept of the human family."

Community Theatre is the setting in which individuals get reconnected to themselves, to other humans and to a larger community. As a theatre for the community, Playback Theatre can highly contribute to the understanding between countries and cultures.

"Ours then is a via negativa – not a collection of skills, but an eradication of blocks." Grotowski, Towards a Poor Theater, 1968

If we imagine that there would be Tarot Cards for Playback Theatre, then one of them would show the following picture and text: In the middle of the card, there is a bridge. The bridge is narrow. It leads over a deep abyss. On the left, we see a rider (a knight or a lady?) and behind the rider, an army of armed soldiers. On the right, there is a natural landscape, trees, a village, people doing their work, some children, animals. Further back: white clouds, a waterfall, some jungle, wideness. In order to cross the bridge, I have to leave all behind: my army, my weapons, my armory, my defense.

If I want to go on, towards freedom, towards joy, I have to cross the bridge or take a detour. I walk alone, naked, with what I am and with my truth.

This card tells you that this is the point in time to let go – that the fighting is over.

Go with hope in your heart and the knowledge that there is more. You are this special part of creation and deeply connected.

Walk yourself out!

This is how we do Playback Theatre:
with the fear of an adult and the secret joy of a child.

This is why we do Playback Theatre:
to discover the courage of an adult and the playfulness of a child.

This is what for we do Playback Theatre:
to be an authentic adult with the open eyes of a child.

In Playback Theatre we don't cover the truth. We want to make the inner reality of the experience of life (the story) visible.

On our way to reconnect to our playfulness and to our creativity, we are confronted with our blocks and with our psychological 'immune system,' because normally we would rather stick to our old patterns to avoid feeling unsure or silly, or to 'losing our face.'

Our blocks from childhood, education and society, our traumas from life, the known and unknown negative inner images and patterns, our unhealthy and false beliefs: it can all be seen and experienced in our acting. We easily feel our inhibitions and our conditioning. We feel the interruption in the flow of energy when we stumble over some stones on the way. We cannot hide and we don't want to hide, because we are asked to be authentic.

There is no 'just jump' into paradise. There are steps in between. The first step is always to become aware that something inhibits us. The second step is a very important one: to accept it. There is a reason for it, but no reason to blame ourselves. This is the respect we owe ourselves. It is the step towards self-love. Out of this growing self-love we get the desire to break through and the courage to jump over our limits. We know that we will have so much more fun without blocks.

In our rehearsals we have the chance to try, because here we can try to jump without getting blamed or left out. In our trainings we are given permission to explore and to risk. By playing, by role-training and by all these beautiful exercises for playbackers, we get so many chances just for trying. Failure or success are not necessarily the focus.

Once in a rehearsal, we practiced doing the opposite of what was normal in difficult situations. Evelyn, feeling guilty even though she hasn't done anything wrong, practiced to exaggerate her behavior.

Coming back after a month from a trip to Europe, she told the story of bringing her practice into real life: "Me and my husband were invited for dinner. We waited at our apartment. Nobody showed up, because the two parties were waiting for each other in different apartments. A simple misunderstanding! We were waiting at the wrong place. Immediately I felt guilty. At this moment, I remembered our session. Finally arriving at the host's apartment, I fell down on my knees and begged loudly and dramatically for forgiveness. Everybody had to laugh! Tension and anger were gone. The dinner was relaxed, delicious and fun after all."

This story was inspiring for all of us.

It was Evelyn's healing moment. Exaggerating the feeling of guilt in an act of drama was her key to becoming conscious of and changing her inner pattern. She was proud and happy. Afterward she was practicing it with a lot of fun and humor wherever she could, until the 'detour through drama' wasn't necessary anymore.

Playback Theatre can be one of the 'doorways to paradise' – with rocks and blocks to overcome! If we don't eradicate at least the biggest blocks, we will keep being busy with them. The blocks on our way through life take a lot of energy to pass by, crawl over or to ignore. They are inhibiting us, holding us back and are consuming our energy. Eradicating our blocks means getting more inner freedom and quietness in our heart. With fewer blocks we are more spontaneous, we are more true and flowing. We need to 'eradicate blocks' in Playback Theatre, because as actors we are asked to be flexible and open.

Marian came to a performance we offered for psychodramatists. She told of a dream: "I was in a church and there was a jam session with jazz and singing. I sang with a lot of fun and very loud and, as usual, pretty false! It was just great. But then I saw a black figure approaching. It laid his hand on my shoulder and whispered: 'This is forbidden.... you sing horrible!' In this moment, in the middle of all those joyful people and the amazing sound, I felt and knew for the first time: I don't want and must not obey this black ghost! I want to sing loud and wrong. From now on jazz! No more only classical music!"

After the story was played back, Marian said, "That was wonderful! It feels like overcoming an input from a family tradition, an input saying 'classical music is the only and best.' Can I join your group? I want to do Playback Theatre!"

This is how Marian became part of our Playback Theatre company – and when I left my company, she became the conductor.

There is another wonderful part to Marian's story: Iwan was chosen for the role of the black figure. When he joined our group, he explained that he cannot sing. Period. He was laughed at when he was a child for singing off-key and decided never to sing again in his life. In the role of the black figure, he experienced his power and pressure onto Marian. But after 'Marian' in the playing back didn't stop singing, he felt helpless. The outcome of being part of this story and consciously experiencing its inner dynamics was awesome for Iwan. He saw that an inner law can be changed, that fun and joy can overcome limits and blocks. Taking Marian's courage as example, he surprised us with his singing in one of our next rehearsals. Iiiiii...... it was really bad!

One story – two blocks exposed and nearly 'removed.' Now they both sang loud and false! It was touching to see them singing their hearts out. Time passed, their singing improved and then it was touching to hear their voices.

The internal patterns stay deep within us. Marian's dream already showed a process of change, but for her it was the teller's actor as confidant who gave the courage to overcome the singing ban. To see a wish put in reality on stage was the 'yes' she needed.

We never can underestimate the impact of the teller's actor, when we watch our own story being played back on stage.

To be chosen for a special role can have a crucial impact on us as actor, like we have seen in Iwan's example. In some way he had a similar history and a similar block as Marian. The teller choosing the roles can be very important for both. Sometimes there are amazing 'fits.' In Playback Theatre this happens often. Roles are not chosen by thinking, but by the unconscious, which chooses not the 'outer' but the 'inner' form.

There are so many possibilities in Playback Theatre to 'work' with our blocks. In one of our rehearsals we focused on body expression. It was an exercise in which we had to move from one end of the room to the other, showing that we have a small container filled with some liquid and were eager not to spill anything. In the following exercise the question was: what happens if you spill something?

All of us western women were showing shame, fear or guilt when the liquid was spilled. Not so our only Balinese man! He put the rest of his machine oil in the same way into the machine as before. He didn't seem to have any blocks, was in flow with what we did and always ready to smile.

To break something, to lose something or to do something wrong has no consequences in his life. There is no need to say, 'I am sorry.' It happened and that's it.

His blocks are different from ours. The block the Balinese carry, for example, is more the subject of 'being alone' or 'being cut off.' It is the fear of being out of the social system, which is family and religion in one. Social life happens on a daily basis within the village and their thousands of ceremonies. To be cut off is horrible, because nobody will talk to you and they turn away from you. Another block is body contact. Among Balinese there is normally no hugging, and rarely do you see them shaking hands. Getting close means intimacy between man and woman and therefore body contact has a different meaning. Can you imagine how difficult it was at the beginning for our Balinese man to do fluid sculptures and pairs and all these exercises with body contact belonging to our rehearsals?

In different countries and in different cultures the blocks or the armor we brought with us will look different. For this reason it is so important to know about other cultures and their belief systems, their habits, and imprints if we want to be a mirror for their stories in an adequate way.

But blocks remain blocks and, to be a playbacker, we need to be flexible and open!

In Playback Theatre our whole being is involved. We are journeying on levels that are deeper than our conscious thinking. We rely not so much on words as on images, on sound and rhythm, on feeling and intuition. Playback Theatre is an improvisational theatre. We never know how a story is going to be played back. We need to join the dance on stage and bring it into beauty from outside in and inside out. We are more powerful actors with fewer blocks.

We may at first feel afraid and shy to find out about our blocks and to overcome them. But, we also feel proud, when we try it and go for it. We feel courageous, when we decide to jump over a limit. We experience the excitement when we jump. We are in a group, and our fellow playbackers not only support us, they also shiver with us and may even clap when we make a leap.

The third of the basic values of Playback Theatre has taken us to the subject of art, of spontaneity and creativity; to our inner child and to the need for eradicating blocks. As actors, engaging in this activity, it provides 'a perfecting of our spirit.' We even could say that artistic activity is 'analogous to divine, free, creative activity.' It is beyond the personal and brings us in touch with the transpersonal. We are trying to reach beyond. We want to re-connect to a source which is available to all.

We are part of a process, which is not only challenging us and taking us to deeper subjects, but which is also making us rich.

One more step of our stairs within Playback Theatre is created – to help us to be rooted and to fly!

COMMUNITY SPIRIT
(AND A MOOD OF POSITIVE PARTICIPATION)
IS TRANSFORMATIONAL

Spirit is something which is not touchable and visible. It cannot be captured with the mind and is hard to describe, because it belongs to another level, as we already have seen before. But, we can experience the spirit of a community.

Community spirit is the expression of this invisible vibration from an idea or a vision, which is touching our hearts. In Playback Theatre our inspiration is transferred to our actions and interactions. It is felt in the atmosphere and it radiates enthusiasm and trust. Something special is happening here! In a performance people can feel this spirit and, by experiencing the playing back of their narratives, a new community spirit can come to life which will be transformational for everybody.

This transformation takes place in the heart of people, by the excitement of the happening on stage, the intimacy of sharing personal matters and the connections growing on a nonverbal level.

We are moving more and more into the transpersonal.

"The problem is how to elicit from every man his maximum spontaneous participation," Moreno, Who Shall Survive, 1937

We already explored in quote one that humans are sensitive beings, mainly living in a deeply disturbed world without real justice and respect for nature, uniqueness and life itself. We also have to be aware that these human beings must be treated carefully, wisely and with clarity. Only if we approach people in a loving, respectful way which gives reasonable direction, is it possible for them to realize that they can take off their social masks without fear and tell their personal stories. This is the spirit of trustworthiness.

We want everybody to take part. The teller's seat is for everyone. People should feel a little different after a performance: lighter, released, touched, inspired, hopeful and more connected. By the concept and the ritual of Playback Theatre we want to create a space where people can participate without fear. Our basic approach is nonjudgmental and caring. We are asking 'only' for 'personal' moments and stories. We are playing them back with compassion and art to show their inner truth. We have no further demands! The core of our task is to find the door to their hearts and to be able to connect them to themselves and others again.

To feel welcomed, seen and appreciated makes people in the audience less inhibited. No experience told is wrong, and there are no bad consequences. You are free to tell something or not. Each narrative can be understood as part of a human being's life. We can find what we all need so badly: we can make friends with being human and overcome our sense of separateness. Change and transformation can happen, because we are meeting on another level.

Our inner attitude of acceptance is like a foundation stone. This will bring people into a mood of positive participation. The more trustworthy the atmosphere, the more the audience can be spontaneous and courageous. As actors we experience a huge benefit: we are given permission to discover what creativity, playfulness and knowledge we already have inside us. By letting ourselves drift into the unknown and dive into 'the skin' of another human being, we gain new perceptions. The highest reward at the end is not really about what we are given; it is about what we become.

We can feel enriched, strong and deeply satisfied after a performance.

This is a contribution to all and to the spirit of the community.

It was my first workshop in America in 1986. During the workshop our group was invited to perform in a home for emotionally disturbed children. They already had a little experience with

Playback Theatre before, and so they were looking forward to this performance. The third story came from a small girl named Lisa. She came to the teller's chair, and we noticed that there was some mumbling among the children. Lisa told about her trip with her mom, her dad and her siblings. They went to Disneyland for the first time. They saw a circus and Lisa loved the funny clown. She also got an ice cream and at the end they made a photo of the whole family with Donald Duck, who had taken her in his arms.

We played the story as told, and Lisa and all the children loved it.

And now comes the wonderful part of the story: the teachers of the home told us later that they were totally surprised that Lisa was telling a story, because normally she was very quiet and didn't say much. Furthermore, she didn't know her parents and she had no brother or sister. She was mostly outside of the group and the children were not especially found of playing with her. But what was even more astonishing for the teachers was to see that, after her courageous act of telling this story, the other children started to play with her more and were in some way caring and loving. It was as if they understood the need and the suffering of not having a family. Since that moment her position in the class changed, and with it, her loneliness. She suddenly was much more integrated. Our group from the workshop was very touched by what the teachers shared with us. In the following talk about our work, we all felt the healing part of Playback Theatre. We had experienced how one story told could change the dynamics of a whole class. We were very proud and mainly so fulfilled that we had been part of this transformative happening.

There are more specific aspects to the atmosphere and the participation of people in Playback Theatre. We will now explore three of them: the first sentence, the benevolent mirror, and the soap bubble.

The First Sentence

The conductor, as the intermediary between audience and team, is the one who in the first step conveys confidence and courage to the audience. Asking for a story is like asking, "What happened to you? Are you doing alright? What has brought joy and what is the pain within your life? What was upsetting you and what was exciting?" It is a loving question, a question that entails this mother-like caring which suggests that you are taken seriously.

This question contains the respect for your experiences in life. When I say: "I would like to hear your story and then play it back to you," it cannot be just a phrase. I must want it and really mean it. This is a commitment and basic promise.

In her book, Jo Salas states that the first thing a conductor should transmit, is the feeling 'that this is a safe place to tell your story.' This sentence – or the meaning of it – has huge consequences. Imagine what this means for another person! This is a big responsibility, for we have to keep our word and be impeccable on that one. Psychologically, this represents a tremendous offer: a space so longed for, a space with no fear of punishment, with the premise of being taken seriously, without being laughed at or ridiculed, has enormous value. To be presented with a space, where I will be seen, heard and understood; where people are interested in me and where I can be of value for others, is fundamentally healing.

If I know I am safe here, I no longer need to be afraid of being cut off, criticized or ashamed. There are no expectations I need to live up to; I can be who I am, and tell what I want without restrictions. This first sentence will have a huge impact.

Most people judge their story as not really important or not interesting enough. We are not used to getting this kind of true attention. We assure to all at the very beginning that everyday stories are all worthy to be told and to be turned into theatre pieces, because they could be of importance for others.

Is that not an awesome message?

Playback Theatre promises to see you as a person worthy of respect and compassion. It says you matter in this world.

The Benevolent Mirror

Playing back is like mirroring. Consciously mirroring is a challenge.

A normal mirror mostly reflects back what we project into it and depending on our mood, we like what we see, or not. We hardly see the truth. Normally our prejudices and assumptions are contained in the mirror we give to others.

In the Tarot deck there is a card called "The Lovers." This card is also a card of decision. Who makes the decision: your heart or your mind? Is our decision to create black or white magic? If the decision is coming from our mind, we are still attached to the materialistic, judging world. If the decision comes from the heart, it serves to expose another dimension, for another aim.

In what kind of mirror do I want to peer: one which is presenting my mistakes or one which enables me to spot my true being?

Our attitude and motivation in Playback Theatre is not to show you your shortcomings and defects, but to show you which special being you are. If we say that we are a mirror, we mean a mirror like the one on the card of the lovers. The two lovers are a mirror for each other and in service for one another. It is a benevolent, loving mirror. The mirror reflects without judgment. The reflected image is wider, more comprehensive and with a deep understanding of life.

If someone can hold a mirror for you without judgment, it is an extraordinary gift. Playback Theatre promises to treat you with respect and since it is a promise, we have to, and want to, keep our word.

Yet, this Tarot card is also about self-love. In the Maya Tarot deck it is the card of the ancestors. Ancestors teach us how to love ourselves and to like us the way we are. It means that we learn how to approach ourselves lovingly.

In Playback Theatre the teller wants to see the truth – his personal truth and the truth of the story. Being allowed to be true, we can accept ourselves better. Looking in a true mirror, shown by the actors, we seem to be better able to love ourselves.

We need to sense and reflect the truth within a teller and his story. Being a true mirror is being like the 'lover' in the Tarot deck. And, the teller will reflect back love to us. We see it in his eyes. Truth at this point is relieving and healing. This is our true service.

For us playbackers it is always a balancing act of treating ourselves with as much empathy as we treat others. Being the mirror for the teller can also be a reflection of ourselves: Did we catch the meaning of the story and/or our role? Where did we get stuck, where did we project? We learn a lot about ourselves.

Sometimes we don't get it quite right and cannot really slip so well into a role or a story. Sometimes we get pretty close to our own feelings and our own experiences. Sometimes we can identify so well with the role that we feel outrageous, lose the team and need the fellow actors to kick us back into the story. Sometimes we can feel the pain or the sadness so strongly, that our tears are dropping on stage. In our company it happened quite often, that an actor had tears running down the cheek. This was no problem – and even wonderful – as long he could shift back to the story and proceed, sometimes just by taking a deep breath.

In order to be a true mirror, a special kind of awareness is needed. We develop a feeling for mirroring. The consciousness of being another person and at the same time ourselves, is our awareness of knowing that we are acting.

The Soap Bubble

In 1991 I created the image of the soap bubble.

On one hand, I knew that Playback Theatre is not therapy. It is theatre! On the other hand, I always felt its healing potential. The soap bubble was an image to describe one of the therapeutic and healing aspects of Playback Theatre.

Being a psychodramatist, I got the important message from J.L. Moreno: "Every true second time is the liberation from the first."

I felt, that the same is happening in Playback Theatre by being a true, respectful mirror and by our playing back!

When 'a story' happens in reality, it is usually loaded with extra energy. We don't know what triggered the extra energy until the story has been told, and we can sense the essence. There was pain or joy; there was excitement, anger, a shock or there was just this more or less 'ordinary' experience within life. Our emotional body has a specific memory, and even we don't remember every detail of the story correctly.

But, the first time is the past and stays with us for some reason.

Normally, a soap bubble bursts. It grows as large as it can, and then it transforms itself into tiny particles which are much lighter, dissolving and dissipating into the air.

Telling a story is picking up the first memory of a specific situation. Remembering and telling gives the bubble "breath." Telling is like giving life to the soap bubble. The teller's perception of a situation, the aura of the experience, and different interpretations, begin to form the whole picture. As the bubble grows and becomes more like a holographic bubble, it contains the real story, yet changes the images told by bringing forth other points of view. The soap bubble allows a look into the kernel of the experience and expands like a panoramic view of all dimensions.

Since the actors listen to the story attentively and with an open heart, they capture the experience like an image within a soap bubble. If they look at the story as soap bubble, it can be a helpful imagery for their perception and their acting. It can make the actors very creative. They have the chance to create a piece of artistic theatre.

The story is told, the bubble is created and "loaded."

The "true second time" can take place now and the tension can be released.

To see your own story (or moment) as a piece of theatre, and to watch yourself in that story on stage, is an exciting experience. We feel the same tension as before. We experience it 'live' again, but at the same time we are the watcher. We have this important part of distance in our perception.

The true second time happens through the playing back and mirroring.

If the playing back, as the second time we live through our story, reveals the first experience on an emotional or spiritual level, the true essence is captured.

The teller is being seen and deeply understood. This is the big release!

The soap bubble can burst and discharge its energy. It will dissolve. There is no need anymore to go back to this moment, to this story.

If we, the team on stage, catch the essence, we catch the main charge of the bubble that is the story, and it can burst and discharge its energy. The story can now be released. This discharging will set energy free, which was trapped in the teller's experience.

For this reason, telling and experiencing the playing back of a story is the true second time, and with it the release. The story and the teller will be transformed.

Transformation means acceptance of the past and inner peace with a part of one's life.

We gain energy. It is like this one experience has no more power. We can let go and gain space for something new or we go on with a new understanding. We gain inner freedom.

The true second time is the liberation from the first!

Discharge is happening with every story or moment told and played back respectfully on stage. This is the healing potential of Playback Theatre!

What is captured will dissolve and fade. What will be left are those unsolved parts within the story, those drops of soapy water which will become a soap bubble some other time.

Since the story is told to many people, it is in some way carried by all, shared by all – and it also calls forth other stories, other soap bubbles. Other stories want to become soap bubbles too!

So many bubbles; so many stories to be told come from within us, from this world, from our human history, and from the 'now' of today's world. Playback Theatre can be a shortcut to expand and dissolve them slowly, to expose the past piece by piece, and make space for hope and for new experiences!

As the next example shows, even unconscious pieces of our human history happen to pop up in our stories. By acting them out on stage, there will be not only a personal soap bubble dissolved, but also a tiny piece of the past.

In our first big performance in a 'real' theatre, I was asking who would be our first storyteller. A young man who sat in the last row raised his hand. Sitting beside me, I asked him when his story took place. Rudy's answer was: "In the Middle Ages." He wasn't aware, that I asked for personal stories, and so we decided to find one together. He chose the age of five for his story. "What happened when you were five years old?" He was silent, but suddenly started to shiver a little: "Ohhhh….." "Yes?" I asked. "Our staircase was dark. I ran downstairs. I wanted to go outside. I didn't see the bucket, fell and screamed. My arm was hurting very much. Later my father took me to the doctor. His office also was a little dark. The doctor said: "You already are a big boy, aren't you?" Than he set my arm without anaesthetization. It was horrible and hurt like hell. But my father was very proud of me." Rudy looked at me saying: "I had forgotten this story," he said shaking his head. "Yes," I answered, "stories from the Middle Ages are not pleasant to remember. They are kind of dark." "My apartment now is very light," he mentioned before he went back to his seat. Some people touched his arm when he passed by.

To act as a benevolent mirror and to dissolve soap bubbles is a gift for all.

There is one exception where we ask for another soap bubble: if the story's end is hopelessness. It can also be a story which is traumatic and where hope, vision, or part of the heart died, or where a big need wasn’t fulfilled. In this moment, we can also offer another ending to ignite a small flame of hope in the teller's life.

Kurt sat on the teller's chair and said: "The small, unimportant word 'butter' in the other story kept staying in my head. Why? Suddenly an old memory came into my mind. I was about six years old and it was during the war. We had very little to eat and mostly I was still hungry after a meal. Once, a soldier was eating bread in front of our house and after he left, I took the little piece which fell down. There was butter on it! Since then and during the whole time of war, I was dreaming of butter, mainly after my mother died and we all were starving."

After the story was played back and ended with a hungry little boy dreaming of butter, I offered him another ending. His eyes started to shine and he said, "The little boy swimming in butter!" The teller's actor, having a huge pile of butter in front of him, jumped in it, eating, smacking and finally saying, "Now I am full!."

Kurt's comment after the enactment: "Oh, yes. Wonderful!"

The whole structure of Playback Theatre is built up carefully and wisely to provide a space for the actors to be able to be spontaneous and creative, and to feel at home in a setting which allows their playfulness and intuition to unfold and flow freely – and for the audience to be encouraged to share life experiences without shame or fear.

At the end of this book, interested playbackers can find a more differentiated exploration and description of the structure and important rules coming along with it.

Our walk takes us now to the ritual of Playback Theatre.

We will experience, that we can find release, connection, trust and renewal in the setting and spirit of Playback Theatre.

The Ritual

The ritual is something which encompasses a basic agreement: we ask – you tell – we play back.

It consists of the repetition of phrases, of sequences. The ritual remains the same throughout each performance. It is the bond of all. It gives clarity, a framework and security. Everybody can feel safe.

To discover its depth and importance, we will look at it from different view points: as the frame of reality and as the doors of magic.

The Frame of Reality

Playback Theatre's concept maintains the ritual during the whole process.

To stay connected to reality, the ritual serves as a frame.

We know that we always come back to the 'here and now.' With this frame and order, we can let go into the unknown and we don't feel lost. It makes us feel safe and encourages us to be spontaneous.

Playback Theatre is principally a journey into the unknown. Sometimes it is like visiting other realities, entering a magical world or dreaming a daydream.

Wherever all the moments and stories told take us during a performance (and of course also in our rehearsals), there is always the reality of the outer frame to keep us grounded.

Time and space are elements which give us orientation in our lives. If we lose that orientation, we normally become afraid. For that reason, the 'outer frame' and its components are so important. They give us the chance to let go of the dimensions of time and space for a short while, so we can enter a timeless space: a space where all stories are welcome. The 'outer frame' holds the link to the reality we left, and brings us back to the safe ground of normal structure and mind control.

We all can feel safe – the audience, the team, and the conductor.

The Doors of Magic

There are many things happening simultaneously, if we look at the dynamics and the process of a performance, and at the different levels and aspects of stories. To further explore the ritual, we were confronted with multiple possibilities.

We decided to name our next view point 'the doors of magic,' and we will describe the possible process of a performance.

Imagine a door: on one side is our so-called reality, while on the other side is the world within human beings, and the world of stories. The frame, anchoring us in reality, allows us to enter the 'doors of magic' and to explore other dimensions.

"Welcome to Playback Theatre!"

Here is the audience. Here is a kind of stage. Here is the conductor and here are the actors and the musician.

There is curiosity, tension and all sorts of feelings.

In the process of Playback Theatre, energy will be building up.

The audience, waiting for the theatre to start, begins to warm up by hearing the first sentences of the conductor, and by the short, personal introduction of the actors and the musician.

The crucial request for 'a moment' to tell vibrates in the room. When the first moment is told and the actors play it back, the 'door of magic' opens up.

More moments are told.

The 'frame of reality' will reduce uncertainty. Tension changes to fascination or interest.

The first invisible threads are woven among people.

The 'door of magic' starts to open up wider when the conductor is looking for a teller to tell a story. Who will be the first story-teller? If a teller is found, we get more curious. The teller comes on stage – now the new direction of the journey will be decided. In which world will he lead us? How are we going to judge it? What feelings are we going to be confronted with? Will we and do we want to understand?

Telling the story is a diving into the story, like going into another world. The conductor is in a special, close relationship with the teller and, at the same time, connected to everybody. He is representing reality, as well as he is the guide into the unknown for all.

The actors are not asking questions, so as not to interrupt the entering in the world of the story's energy. The actors stand up when they are chosen for a role. To choose roles is an exciting part. Actors are in this moment in a paradoxical situation: chosen to "be" somebody else, but still standing. Standing up helps them to switch in their 'new skin.' While standing, they are highly focused on their role and on the energy of the story.

They are chosen for their role according to the teller's internal picture, the one that represents best the energy of this particular role, no matter if man or woman.

Unbelievable, incredible matches can occur concerning personal backgrounds or individual experiences.

As actors we know sometimes intuitively that we will be chosen for a specific role.

The interview is finished; the story is told. The conductor says "Lets watch!," which means, "Let's see your story come alive, becoming three- or four-dimensional." "Let's watch" is like a magical spell, an "Open Sesame." With these words, the conductor hands the story over to the actors and the musician.

Now he is the one who is watching, close to the teller and in eye-contact with the audience. No one interrupts, because another 'door of magic' is opening up.

The musician starts to play some sounds, and it is like the spirit of the story is already floating in the room while the actors set the stage. They find their spot on stage, and some dynamics of the story already become visible through their body postures. It looks like an image or the title of the story. No words. No movement yet.

No sounds, except the music of the musician.

The actors stay like frozen statues on stage for a moment. This means we are ready. In different intensities, they all are in some way tuned into the reality of the teller's story, already a little linked by the threads between their characters. Tension grows. The music stops. The playing back of the story begins. Nobody knows how the story is going to be played back. The dynamic of the play unfolds by itself.

The actors need to develop the story together, and together they must find an ending. During their play they are supported by the musician, who is part of the team; music can express what cannot be spoken. Energies are transformed into sound, transcending the limitations of words. Music enhances the story's emotional quality. It touches our feelings and our hearts. Music connects the actors to one another and coalesces their movements, and weaves an unknown emotional net among people. Music is a wonderful gift in Playback Theatre. We are carried by a flow and cannot help but tune in. The musician underlines and shapes the actors' expression and dynamics within their play. Music links all and everything, and is bringing in another dimension, enlarging the space and changing feelings into a sound beyond.

Like it's unfolding a multitude of inner realities, the whole room begins to vibrate. It could be like a dream sequence. While acting on this level, the actors are no more in their ordinary consciousness; their perception and spontaneous actions open up to different channels.

However we play back the story, we do it as a team, because we have to do it together. It is a dance of following, standing back and taking action.

The conductor and the teller are watching. This phase is very intense for the teller and a lot is happening inside of him. Therefore it is important that the conductor keeps his inner connection to him.

The story ends with maybe a last word from the teller's actor or a touch of music.

The story is played back. The 'doors of magic' are slowly closed. The actors give the story back to the teller with their eyes. Their eyes show their sharing of feelings, their empathy and love for the teller and the experience. This look expresses: "I was with you. This is what I could do for you." That's how they let go of their roles. Mostly the actors are still connected in a subtle way with the teller, the story or the role. In this moment they are quite vulnerable, because they are asking themselves: "Was I good?," which means "Did I pass the test?," "Did I fulfill my role for the good of the teller?," "Was I in tune with the energy of the team?" and “Did I contribute enough?"

There is no other theatre where a person can learn such depth and richness about life by joyful playing. If we are taking the role to be a Playback Theatre actor seriously, we have an incredible chance to explore in so many different ways what it means to be human and to open our deepest core. We free and enrich ourselves by playing. We exchange experiences and gain knowledge.

The conductor's 'check-back' with the teller follows. This gives the teller the opportunity to express something, to share what he experienced, and also to be able to return to this reality, because he has to go back to his seat.

In this moment, the teller is very vulnerable. As teller we have shown something intimate – maybe something secret – but at least something (very) personal. That's why the teller needs our loving inner attitude of respect, as well as the frame of Playback Theatre's ritual to come back to reality.

Most tellers don't say much; some are crying because they are moved by being so deeply understood. Some just say "Thank you," while some laugh and say, "I will remember this!" Some say "This part was different for me," and tell about the difference. This correction is important for the teller for to keep it 'his' story. We listen to it, hear it and integrate it in the inner image of the story. But, there is no correction by playing it back differently. We always want to honor the spontaneous acting of the performers, because they have done their best. To ask them to play the correct version, would in some way diminish what they have done before and could mean their effort was "not good enough." To correct a story may improve its accuracy, but not the playfulness and spontaneity of the actors. In all cases the teller is normally fine by having the opportunity to convey the difference.

There only is this one exception we have already have looked at: if the story is ending with deep despair, we can offer another ending. This second soap bubble is not to create a "happy ending," but for some new perspective in the teller's life. But, in this instance it is so important that the new ending is always the teller's own image or solution!

After this enactment there is another check back with the teller and the ritual goes on.

The conductor thanks the teller. The story has been honored.

The teller goes back to his chair. He is within himself, but also confronted with the presence of other people.

A silent knowledge about something personal, about someone, touches the hearts and connects all those who are present, no matter how close or distant we felt to the story we witnessed. Another story of someone's life was shared, another 'truth' was revealed, another bit of wisdom was captured in an experience we can learn from.

This story has been played back. This is the call for everybody to return to ourselves. In reality, we see that there is a stage with a team, and there is an audience.

We pass through 'the door of magic,' finding ourselves back in the 'frame of reality.' "Reality" is still here, and the ritual will continue.

Another story will be played back. The audience members wonder: could or shall it be mine? The magic doors will open again.

The ritual starts again.

In the audience, the atmosphere has a special vibe. That story has been touching other stories, other lives. A story touching deeper levels of life – the death of a child, or the joy of having been able to end a fight with a friend, or lifting a secret which weighed heavily on our hearts – strengthens the connection among people, because the hearts have been opening up. This is the moment when the performers look at each other so as to say: This is what we are meant for!

We know there is a red thread, a connection between these stories. We may never be able to research or find out why they pop up, but they do pop up. Consciously or from the unconscious, compensating or supporting each other, calling for one another or bringing in a new impulse – the red thread is ever-present and connects us all.

The unconscious always wants to communicate. The communication happens through symbols or images. Life's wisdom and challenge weaves the pattern with a single red thread.

When the last story has been told and the time agreed upon is over, the team finds an ending to round up the performance. It might be an appreciation of all experiences told. The performance has come to its definite end. The magical doors on stage are closed.

We all go back in our lives, a little more connected and enriched, hopefully warm in our hearts, and maybe contemplative.

In the first citation of quote four we have experienced the transformative quality of the spirit in Playback Theatre, which also gets visible in the second citation.

"A love ethic has nothing to do with sentimental feelings or tribal connections. Rather it is a last attempt at generating a sense of agency among a downtrodden people." West, Race Matters, 1993

The common definition of ethics is: a branch of philosophy dealing with values relating to human conduct. They may be understood as a set of moral principles that enable us to put our general understanding of well-being into practice in ways that are suitable to each occasion.

Ethics in Playback Theatre take another viewpoint.

A love ethic has not so much to do with moral principles as it does with the equality and worth of all human beings. Personal ethics have to do with integrity, fairness and truth.

As we already know, Jonathan Fox first called Playback Theatre "Theatre of Love." Love does not judge – this is the meaning of love in Playback Theatre. A love ethic is a love which opens up to everybody. The mind doesn't understand everything and is very fast with assumptions, criticisms and judgments of all kinds. We can't help it in the moment, but the heart can help. The heart can teach us. Every time, for example, when I go to a performance or a Playback Theatre workshop the same thing happens: I hear my own internal comments right away. But it doesn't take long for everything to change. In no other situations have I experienced so much lasting and loving acceptance as in Playback Theatre.

A love ethic doesn't exclude, but wants to include. Playback Theatre admits that everybody has a worthwhile story and gives everybody the chance to be a teller. Our ethics are not moral issues, but are instead a loving attitude towards the person who is willing to share his story in front of a whole audience.

Ethics can be a subject in many stories: in stories of man and woman, of teacher and pupils, in love affairs, and in stories of people with a different color of skin. In Playback Theatre we want to put a love ethic above moral issues and judgments.

"There once was a woman on the teller's chair who told her story about secretly going into her seventeen-year-old daughter's room and reading her whole dairy with all the intimate details! Nobody saw her, but she 'felt strange' afterward. Now she knew what was going on outside and inside her daughter. She never told her."

From a moral point of view we could say: "Not correct!" But, in Playback Theatre we want to look at a human being in all its facets. How disconnected from her daughter and how desperate or unsatisfied must a mother be, to do what felt so 'strange' afterward. In our playing back we can share for example the despair or suffering. If we can catch some of the background feelings and reasons, we will give release.

We have tellers who want to demonstrate how amazing they are or tellers who want to bluff with an extraordinary event – why not let them? Isn't there a hidden need? There might be a teller whose story goes so much against our own morals, that they are difficult for us to accept and to play back – we still can try to convey their inner truth, without needing to bring our personal opinion in. We don't know if telling this story is a courageous admission of a hidden truth, or the first step of being honest to himself and others?

We can show our personal ethics by acting according to Playback Theatre's basic values. Ethic is love and respect. We are able to show respect to another person, even when our morals are different. It is reaching down to other sources. Then it can become a shared experience of something human. Then it is such a bliss to see the teller and the audience being touched!

Social change happens in those small steps, which are done by listening carefully and finding the hidden message. Change takes place in our perception, in the perception of the people in the audience and of the teller. Playback Theatre has 'the good for all' in mind. This is easily said, but only done if we are consciously developing a fuller understanding of what it is to flourish. The flowering of the human spirit, which is part of Playback Theatre's vision, will not only happen within the individual, but will also grow in communities and finally, hopefully, in the world. The flowering will touch our unconscious or hidden longing, slowly or sometimes abruptly.

Freedom is a dangerous word. We all want it and long for it, but at the same time, it triggers real fear: What, who, how am I, when I am free? To cope with this unstructured space seems a little more difficult than the idea of it. Playback Theatre comprises this fear and how to overcome it. We offer a space of hope and warmth for everybody. The magical level of the transformative atmosphere in Playback Theatre is our ethical base, shown in our actions and attitude.

Social change and transformation will happen slowly, and we contribute to it in our own way and with the multiple possibilities we are able to bring in through Playback Theatre. Our potential is big – and it is even bigger if we manage to support and to inspire each other in our company or community. The best approach is to start to practice a love ethic with ourselves and then to enlarge it to our fellow playbackers. Transformation happens deep within people, on a level without words. It is the spirit of Playback Theatre which makes the difference. The benevolent atmosphere can loosen tongues and open hearts; fulfillment of a deep need is its promise.

Playback Theatre provides one more step towards a humanity where we can experience safety and hope from connectedness, and the individual is contained and can flourish.

Now we will discover the fifth and final quote on basic values.

WE CAN CONNECT TO A "MUSIC"
BEYOND OUR IMMEDIATE CONCERNS
THAT WILL BRING PEACE AND JOY

It was Pythagoras who first called heaven 'kosmos,' because it is "perfect, and 'adorned' with infinite beauty." "The music" we connect with is a music of the cosmos or the universe. It is full of sound and colors.

We, as human beings are surrounded by a universe of which we know little. The centers of sense perception within ourselves are not developed sufficiently to respond to the subtle rates of vibration of which that universe is composed. In fact, there are innumerable sounds which cannot be heard, colors which cannot be seen – as well as flavors which cannot be tasted or odors which cannot be smelled.

So how can we connect to something which is not visible, not touchable and we are not able to catch with our senses?

How do we describe something which is not really explainable, not visible to our eyes and is difficult to describe directly with language? How to write about "the music?"

If we are together with our beloved and everything is so good, we say, "I am in heaven!" If we eat something delicious, we say, "This food tastes heavenly!" They are experiences of bliss, of Pythagoras' heavenly cosmos. Yes, that's what this "music" feels like: heaven.

There is no direct way to describe the music of Playback Theatre. We only find answers by detours and by the citations within this quote.

Our small excursions take us through the known and unknown. To capture this subject only with our mind is not possible, because some things can not be easily understood. To talk (or to write!) about "the music" can bring our mind to its limit – but not our heart! We have a feeling for what lays beyond.

'Detour one' takes us to a small part of today's immense science of the brain. Knowing that science is changing and expanding constantly, I still want to share one interesting aspect:

Our brain has two hemispheres, and they function very differently.

Every bit of information from all our senses streams into our brain and explodes into an enormous collage of the present moment. The left hemisphere thinks in a linear and methodical way, picking out details, categorizing and organizing all the information and associating it with the past and whatever we have learned. The left brain then projects those associations to the future with all possibilities. Left hemisphere thinks in language. It makes the connection of the inner and the outer world. It is where our brain-chatter comes from. It has consciousness about our being. At the same time, we lose connection to the whole and this is where our separation happens.

The right hemisphere thinks in pictures and cares about different things – it is in some ways like a different personality and picks up what it sounds like, looks like, tastes like and feels like. With the consciousness of our right hemisphere we are an energetic being. We connect to the energy around us. We can feel our connections and can have the experience that we are one human family. In this moment there is no separation, no left-brain chatter.

It's like our inner radio changed the channel.

If the two hemispheres were balanced and in optimal cooperation, we would perceive and connect to the world in a different, more flexible way. We might be more conscious about "the music."

With the second detour, we have a quick look at people who cannot hear: they can 'hear' sounds by touching and even by watching. They are able to feel the vibrations with the body. Our body is therefore a resonating box!

Our next detour brings a lot of further insight: we will have a short look back into history.

It is said that Moses heard the cosmic music when he received the tablets on Mount Sinai, or that men can hear the music on the point of death, revealing the highest reality of the cosmos.

Now we need to switch back to Pythagoras: Pythagoras is know as the discoverer of the basic, constitutional intervals of music. The legend tells that Pythagoras discovered the so called 'harmonioi' in a blacksmith's shop – the sound of a hammer hitting the ambos. His further research led to an enormous discovery. In short, these intervals are the mathematical matrix for all music! Music is simply mathematics! Pythagoras also said that the movements of the planets don't make sound, but that the planets themselves are the music and don't need an outside medium to be music. Mathematics shows that these basic intervals originate in the harmony of the spheres. They are the matrix for all further calculations within science, architecture and nature; valid since the ancient world and still valid today!

Every musician or music theorist can easily explain to an ordinary person that the structures of music are plain mathematics. All elements of music and all processes within music are explainable with mathematics or mathematical cycles!

Relying on Pythagoras's discovery and knowledge, the Roman philosopher Boethius then differentiated three types of music: the music of instruments, the music of the human body and soul, and the music of the spheres or the cosmos.

This brings us back on our walk and closer to "the music."

The music of the cosmos is present everywhere and governs all temporal cycles such as the seasons, biological cycles, and all the rhythms of nature. In my understanding the mathematics found in music could also mean that the matrix of the inaudible music of the spheres is contained in all. Therefore the music of the instruments and of humans would be a duplicate, a reproduction of the original matrix! This is where our link could originate.

Since this is still theory, we had better move on to experience: How do we experience the music?

In my life I was so lucky to have some experiences of "the music."

In my American Indian training in the Deer Tribe in Switzerland, I joined a Sweet Sundance (without piercing). The earth drum, deep and regular, never stopped. After three days and three nights dancing, forwards and backwards to the tree in the center, with little sleep and only drinking water, I felt exhausted. But in this moment, when we all stood together at the very end, I was overwhelmed. It's hard to describe what I experienced. Standing in this circle, I felt like my feet were deeply anchored in the earth and at the same time I experienced a kind of freedom and lightness as if I could fly. My heart was so open seeing myself connected with all the others – and even with all humans. I knew that life takes good care of me, and of all. We stood silent, together, in a vibrant space, nourished by a well of no name. I also felt this connectedness many times in Playback Theatre.

One example was in a three-day workshop with Veronica Needa in Singapore. We were people of eight different countries and we spoke at least twelve native languages. At the beginning I watched myself sometimes judging others; my brain was giving comments about what should or should not happen. But within a short time, all those details got so unimportant. All the different cultures appearing in the stories took me on to another level, like in a world of fairy tales. What was so amazing was that we could go beyond words and just feel the power of the beauty of what we were doing. I could dive into the souls of others, and like so often in Playback Theatre, my heart was wide open. At the end we were fulfilled and light from tears, laughter and this special kind of love for one another, which needs no words.

"The music" – as an unconditional acceptance we had for each other – was like a healing warm bath; like connecting threads passing the borders of cultures.

Quote five wants to bring us closer to transcendence, to something unseen, something "Divine."

We feel that we can connect to this heavenly space through the music.

In the universe, a cosmic symphony is being played and we all can be plugged into it. Human beings are part of the cosmic music. We belong to the whole. We are vibrating beings and everything about us is frequency.

I couldn't resist writing a little poem:

Sounds of origin, vibrations of the universe
supporting the tunes of every single being
Invisible net growing
linking single songs
into harmony
refining, enriching itself
A concert composed of the uniqueness of each
A symphony expressed in melodies for the joy of life
An ecstasy about being alive – a minuet of cheerfulness
Beyond our worries is quietness and peace –
Experience of bliss.

Each one of us came into this world with a unique composition of frequency. We could call it 'our song.' But through no fault of our own, our song often gets distorted. It becomes more like noise. Most humans don't sound like an individual song or like a harmonious composition. For so many people, the mind makes so much noise that it's impossible to hear their own sweet music. There seems to be a great cacophony on this planet.

Pythagoreans thought that human beings fail to hear these divine melodies, because their souls are enmeshed in the illusion of material existence.

In Playback Theatre's loving atmosphere, where we feel that we can open up, there is a space to rediscover our own notes again and have a possibility to experience how it is when people 'make music together.'

If we talk about "a music which lays beyond," we mean a frequency of harmony, of peacefulness. Sometimes it is even more like silence. We get embodied by it, we can sink in it and melt with it. On this level there is no fear anymore, no tension, no rational thinking. This is the space of just being part of the bigger whole without getting lost. Everything that is happening just seems to fit. All is in its right place and timing. With this perception we feel perfect, whole and beautiful. There is peace.

We get a feeling of what it means to all be connected. The peace we experience in this moment is the peace which lays beyond our normal experiences, beyond our mind, beyond our ego.

"The music" of quote five is on this frequency. It is entering into our heart. That is where we feel it, where we get touched.

Transcendental spaces are not 'somewhere out there' – we can find them in our innermost core, in the sanctum of all life. This frequency or music lies beyond our worries.

Transferring these dynamics to Playback Theatre, I see a single being expressing a part of his life in tunes (telling a story). A variety of melodies and other tunes start vibrating with it. We tune in, some more, some less, some high, some low. Not only the actors and the audience pick up the individual frequency, but also something transpersonal will swing with this person's open heart and tune into the vibrations of all those present. This is music! New tunes will chime in (other stories are told), and other frequencies will be explored. Each narrative brings out another melody. Each common concert (each performance) is connected in a different intensity and on different levels with the infinite music of our origin. This is how we can hear our own human music in accordance with the matrix of the universe. The music is connecting us on a level which cannot be expressed.

One of my friends, Ruth, was a teller in a performance and later told me of her experience: "Actually, I didn't want to tell a story. But all at once I found myself walking forward like in trance. It seemed like my body wanted it. On the teller's chair I asked myself: What shall I tell? I didn't know. I looked in the audience and saw many of my 'playback-children.' Immediately my heart opened wide and I felt all the hope for a better understanding among people we shared in some of our stories. Then I started to speak: 'Once there was a little girl with wishes and dreams of a peaceful world – not a world with war, with people and children suffering so much as in those days of the world war. She hoped there would be no more war. But when she grew older, she experienced that the world had not gotten better, but still was dark. She decided not to give birth to children in an unpleasant world. But she fell in love, married and had a daughter and a son. When her daughter said she didn't want children, it was a release. But the daughter fell in love, married and had two children. That is how the little girl became a grandmother with two granddaughters. And now she has so much joy to watch them, to be and to play with them. They are so alive and hopeful. I know, that life will go on and with it our hope for less destruction.' I had tears in my eyes, and I saw that others in the audience also had tears in their eyes."

This story has many layers. "The music beyond" can be felt as a deeply connecting sadness, and as the deepest hope of a survival which is more than just survival. It becomes a hope, the beauty of a vision of the world as it was meant to be, replacing the ruination which took over: a hope which speaks for the wisdom of life itself.

This story happened to be the last one in the performance, and a warm feeling of knowing and connection was vibrating in the room. It was a moment the music could be heard.

The world of stories can takes us somehow into the uncertainty of their origin, to the collective or to where everything is linked. Since the concept and the process of Playback Theatre invites the unseen to take part, the transpersonal space can shine through and reach our hearts.

Elisabeth's story was a story about death: "One of my closest friends has cancer and is going to die soon. I accompanied her in her process. She didn't want any treatment or chemotherapy. She was very brave. In the last phase of her illness, fear and pain started to take over. She knew how the end was going to be, and rather wanted to die. She decided to go to a clinic in Switzerland, where this is possible if you are terminally ill. She asked me to be there with her husband and also to stay there for the next seventy two days as it is practiced in Buddhism. My clear answer was "yes." I drove to this clinic and prepared everything in detail with the staff there.... they were so loving!

It was a rainy, gray day and I was waiting. They did not come! Elisabeth told me on the phone that, in the moment she was ready to leave, she suddenly was overwhelmed with love and respect for life. She immediately knew that she wanted to fulfill her life and to live through all the experiences life was offering to her. I understood. I admired her courage and felt the rightness of her personal decision. I was deeply touched. I felt fate for universal laws. I drove back, exhausted, but calm and in inner peace with life and death. I felt a strong sense of trust and I was filled with love. I knew that she was in good hands with her doctor. I knew that she was in good company with her husband. And I knew that she will be in good hands after death.... And I will accompany her from far away."

Many people cried. We all felt close. We shared a space in which all aspects of life were accepted: a space of trust, courage and surrender. It was a space of light, where we are able to overcome fear and where we can hear the music inside our hearts.

"When I visit communities, I frequently ask, 'How do you celebrate?' If they say, 'We don't celebrate,' then I know the community risks death." Vanier, Community & Growth, 1993

Celebration has something to do with respect, with joy and with sacredness.

It is not partying. Celebration is an expression of the value of something.

We celebrate ourselves (hopefully at least our own birthday), we celebrate a common idea (for example in a religious context or similar), we celebrate a happening (such as a wedding, the first performance, the birth of a child), and we can also celebrate death. Because we celebrate life, a human being whose life has come to an end, who has lived life as best as she could, can also be celebrated.

The focus in this citation again points to community. It's about "life together," and that living together is a challenge and can be painful, but is at the same time a marvelous adventure. It is like holding a diamond towards the light and by rotating it, being able to see all the different ways in which it shines and reflects the light. Like this, celebration within the community becomes a source for life and wisdom. Those celebrations give meaning and show the value of living and pursuing life in a community.

There is always joy and honor for the common vision.

If there is no reason for celebrating, something fundamental gets lost. The community will fall apart, because the inner connection, the sense or the vision is lost. The 'why' is lost. The 'why' in a real community makes people more loving. They are connected by a 'spiritual' bond. The individual knows of the importance of the community. People are rooted in a transcendent order or in a divine reason. There is a spontaneous internal appreciation of everybody. All have the call to contribute to it.

If this is lost and of no more value, nobody seems to care anymore. There is no need for anything anymore. Each single member goes his own way, protects himself and deals with life alone. Individuals might get lost. Who cares? Not my business! And all hide their desire for togetherness, for the better. Everybody is cheating himself.

With each playing back of a moment or a story in Playback Theatre, we celebrate a piece of somebody's life. Each moment told is worth a theatre piece!

We join each meeting, workshop or event in Playback Theatre because it's exciting.

If we can remember the call of Playback Theatre, we will feel a sort of coming home. We honor what we are doing.

If we start fighting each other about rigid concepts and formalism, we forget what brought us together originally. We put a materialistic concept above a more human and spirit-conducted base, where meaning, common growth and creativity are primary.

We need structure, but the structure should be like a frame in which individuals can dance, explore and grow. A worthwhile structure demands dialogue as basic interaction. A rigid structure immediately triggers what we wanted to overcome and inhibits our original drive.

Playback Theatre's concept challenges us to believe in what we are doing:

We have good reasons to celebrate!

A person is "transversed by the solicitations of actual grace." Maritain, Integral Humanism, 1968

When we are touched by what is happening in Playback Theatre, we have a feeling of thankfulness. If we feel seen and worthwhile and if we can be each others' confidants, we get that unspeakable feeling of gratefulness. We feel blessed and it makes us soft and ready to open our hearts for more. Reality seems to enlarge and to extend to an experience of multiple connections. At the same time, by looking into the wideness of the world, we are once again conscious of the fact that we cannot control life. We feel the awe for life itself. This respect makes us humble. It gives us reason to be in connection with the unseen, to accept the cosmic plan and to strive for our own completion by taking our part in the whole.

If we can dance in life like 'the fool,' we will be this unique part and possess the modesty needed for effective, two-tracked communication: the two-way contact with infinity and the transpersonal.

Playback Theatre is the biggest challenge in my life, and the most beautiful one. It is about me – which is good; and it's about more than me – which is very good. I learn to bend down to myself and to creation.

Playbackers are human beings, willing to explore and change, whose drive is to get fulfillment by connecting their individual spontaneity and creativity and their own uniqueness with others – to create magic, connection, truth and art with courage on stage – as an act of service for themselves and others, and to celebrate life as it is.

"The dance ritual was a means of entering the Unseen by force: a two-way contact with the divine, both persuading and being inspired." Hunniger, The Origin of Theatre, 1955

The idea of 'Creation' or 'God' flows in the smaller 'gods' – like humans – existing in many small, single or unique parts. The idea concentrates and then flows back into its origin. This is a peculiar, special dynamic. In this way a two-way contact can take place. In a ritual 'the Unseen' captures the vibe of our energy and we can be in tune. We hear or intuitively feel, that 'the Unseen' is calling us, persuading us, saying: "Please, take something from me!"

We can't sit there passively and wait for God to kiss us. We must attract inspiration, and we need to give something also. It's a two-way trade! We have to take our responsibility. We have to make some steps towards it – and we cannot go straight into it.

As we have seen, the ritual in Playback Theatre gives an important frame. Within that frame a little door opens to something within us which is congruent to our rightness and our longing. Playback Theatre opens a space in which there is room for humanness. Our stage is not sealed; it is a free-flowing area. It reflects and mirrors the experiences of humans as condensed theatre pieces, and lets them flow back again through humans into the world.

The essence of the vision of Playback Theatre has a high potential for 'the Unseen' to manifest on stage. Our part is to be receptive and accessible, which means open and ready – maybe patient, because we don't know what will happen and when.

We give by devoting ourselves to something higher, to something that surpasses our ego. We are opening up, being consciously courageous of letting go and willing to be guided – this is our offer for the contact with the divine.

Giving trust and courage to this knowledge and process, 'the Unseen' will reply with joy! In this answer we will experience something like delight.

We will be inspired, and with that inspiration we can go beyond our individual realities, together.

The ritual of Playback Theatre opens the door for everybody to go beyond: the audience, the actors, the musician and the conductor. And it is the same ritual which holds the frame to reality, the way back to the here and now, back to where we are now, back to life.

"When the ceremony was over, everybody felt a great deal better, for it had been a day of fun. They were better able now to see the greenness of the world, the wideness of the sacred day, the colors of the earth." Neihardt, Black Elk Speaks, 1932

The inspiration we feel, the fun of cooperating and seeing beyond will make us alive. By letting people be human and by accepting their story as worthwhile, a seed is planted, a color invented, a sound created.

We all can see the red of a rose!

There is a huge difference between seeing 'the red of a rose' and describing 'the red of a rose.' The description will come out of our head, but not out of experience. It will always be a picture! Playback Theatre allows us to see and experience the red by being touched by the pain, the sadness, the joy, the fun and all the feelings which come forth through the stories told.

Tiki, a Balinese woman, told her first story. It was a threatening story!

"I was downtown in the main city with my husband and a friend. We wanted to go for dinner. In the basement of our favorite restaurant all the tables, except one, were busy. My husband suggested to go upstairs where it was more quiet. I didn't want to, but as a good Balinese wife I agreed. The waiter came and we ordered our food. Suddenly a big detonation was happening. The restaurant was shaken, people were screaming and smoke was all over. We wanted to rush downstairs, but there were no more stairs leading downwards. The waiter was laying dead on the upper steps. We couldn't breathe anymore. We started to shout out of the window. There was chaos everywhere and at first nobody heard us. 'I am going to die,' I thought. And in this moment a prayer came from deep within my heart: 'Please, God, do not let me die now. I just got my daughter back after so many years and I must be with her.' There was a man noticing us up there. They tried to find a way to help us down. Finally we succeeded to get down, hardly being able to breathe. We survived."

Tiki cried.

After a few moments, she told us that since she got married again, she had to leave her daughter with her first husband, according to family laws in Bali. After twelve years of fighting, she finally could take her home.

The story was about the first bombing in Bali where many people got killed.

What made 'the music to be heard' was not the happy ending, nor only getting closer to one another by sharing the fear of destruction and violence, but the way the actors could transfer an attitude of respect towards life, a surrender to the higher powers within the deep honesty which was laying in Tiki's prayer.

The silence afterward was full of loving eyes, some with tears. It was like being together on a boat after a storm, looking in the wideness of the sky and watching the clouds drifting on a wide horizon. The connectedness was strong. There was no need for words.

It is not possible to describe "the music" in words. It's only possible to feel it in the moment or to experience its outcome when you return to reality and see the beauty of it. It is on this level we realize once more that we do not have real control over life. The universe has its own way of reaching completion. It is on this level where we can see the non-judgmental beauty of creation which we are part of.

Having been touched by "the music," we know why we must deal differently with one another. "The music" carries the important message to us: that we can be inventive, innovative and creative spirits with an independent, individual mind and a differentiated emotional body. Since each one is worthwhile, everybody can contribute.

"Not classes, 'culture circles;' not pupils, 'group participants;' not lecture, 'dialogue.' "
Freire, Education for Critical Conscious-ness, 1973

Freire believes and demonstrates that liberating education and authentic communication are possible. Simply said, his focus and his subject are concerned with the process toward equality and rightness. All humans are people of worth. Human beings are 'with,' not 'in' the world, and are 'beings of relationships.' People must get out of the role of objects with no thinking or opinion on their own and must to become subjects with their own brain and their own destiny. To be human is to engage in relationships with others and with the world. Relationships with the world are plural in nature. Freire votes "against producing pupils who conform to anonymous authorities," adapting a self which is not authentic. We need a critical consciousness as the motor of cultural emancipation and transition. Transition is change, and change might be difficult, but to see the 'mystery' of change is worthwhile.

Freire's requisitions are very much in accordance with the concept of Playback Theatre. They remind us again of our focus, and with it, of the specific value of Playback Theatre: we go beyond, and we set a new frame for connection, inter-relationship and social change.

The world is an amazing place! The whole world and all the stories of humans are our classroom. Our attitude towards people comes from a positive stance and is loving, humble and communicative. All human beings are not objects, but subjects, which are important and merit active respect. We all have a worthwhile story! We seek humanity with our perception and our actions. Our connection to people is through activity – we are listening and playing back. We see that stories have an impact on others. We know that we must gain an awareness of social and cultural contexts of the stories told. Our spirit must be flexible, if we want to find the collective wisdom of stories.

An open mind, with the capability of discrimination, allows us to acknowledge and honor our diversity. We learn to make the right decisions for reaching out into the world. By sharing and discussing we realize that we are not only capable of dialogue, but also how empowering this is. We can discuss our different positions, but we don't want to crush each other.

Since by now Playback Theatre is all over the world, we have and need an intercultural communication. We turn away from globalization, but we tune in to the vocabulary universe.

All this cannot be taught theoretically.

This can only be taught by giving the opportunity of experience.

We have to drop many old patterns of learning and teaching. No more punishment and reward. We learn best with an open mind, heart and body, and that is what we teach those who want to be playbackers. It means preparing a playful knowledge base using exercises and giving hints, ideas or images. It means being open for dialogue, constructive feedback and discussions.

Jonathan Fox never was critical of what we did in our exercises in our rehearsals. If he saw somebody having difficulties with expression, or if he wanted another kind of acting, or if what we did was not appropriate, he just invented a new exercise. It was sometimes obvious that this different approach was about correction. Also, he made simple drawings, which we quickly tried to copy in our notebooks. But afterward, they only made sense when we understood the meaning, the depth and the dynamics of the figures. He presented us images which were far from being only facts. It made a deep impression on me. I saw that nobody ever got hurt or blamed. It always was encouraging and so much fun. We learned as a group and in a different way how to be conscious, what it meant to do Playback Theatre. This is how I learned to teach: to be creative and nonjudgmental as a teacher.

"Turner uses term 'liminal' to refer to the 'creative zone' in the social drama when the rules are in limbo. What happens in the liminal state is a future." Turner, From Ritual to Theatre: the Human Seriousness of Play, 1981

There is no way to jump into "paradise." To change our future into one that is more worthwhile can sometimes leave us shaken. We might feel anxious, unsure, or even frightened. We want to hold onto the old, known structures. Anger might come up. All the things that hold us back, the "blocks," fight for their survival. It looks like chaos all over. But we also want to go on, out of the discomforting 'scenery,' out of the liminal. The space of being in between is at the same time the zone where we get in touch with our resources and our creativity. In the creative zone we get pressured and moved. Change is happening by unknown reasons and is in fact out of our control. We are still within "God's experiment" and have no overview of Creation. Change is conducted by sudden insights, by a touch of our heart and by impulses from creativity itself. Creativity always seeks an optimal solution for an idea or hope. The images and feelings within this moment or phase will be the guide for the future.

As we have seen before, the ritualistic way in which Playback Theatre happens gives structure and security. When the rules are in limbo, it is at the same time the doorway to the "creative zone." We get an idea of how and what we want and need. The trouble and the beauty we experience in the creative zone comes to the surface. We desire a new way of living and interacting. We can catch a vision, a new hope. We "see" how it could go on. We are aware in our consciousness that everybody is going through their own process of life, and we don't need to direct the others. But, we are touched by an archetypical image. The joy and relief which comes along with it, is different then what we call happiness. It is the experience of a special energy. We realize that we may have a new focus, a feeling for a common truth which is existential. The impulse for the future is set.

In Playback Theatre it seems that we are dancing. It is a dance with its own rules, with an unknown source guiding us, surpassing the single actor.

The actors on stage must cooperate and are dependent on one another to play back the story. The connection to the story, to what is told, to reality, is present. They are not getting lost, because they have a focus: to bring the story forth, together, for the teller. It makes sense. It is something which is worth working for. But, they are not told how to play this story back. They have skills, but they must take action in a different way.

As actors, we must try to dance a dance we heard of, but which could not really be taught. There is a vibration of excitement, a letting go, a trust in one another and no thinking. This is the moment when something happens, which we could call a "magic dance." We start acting on another level and suddenly we seem to know how to "dance." Our dance floor is trust – the trust we have in this theatre, in one another and in ourselves. Creativity is our "dance master." We dance, linked by energy, the story and our focus. This is what we call the trance of the actors. If this happens (and if only to a certain degree) we know why Playback Theatre is sometimes called magic. When the dance is over, the story played back, we just feel fulfilled.

In Playback Theatre we want to connect people. Our intention is to transcend superficial differences that divide us: race, religion, politics, beliefs and culture.

The trance of the actors can lead everybody into a daydream-like state. The story, portrayed by the actors as a timeless condition, an eternal now, as a moment in and out of time, gathers everyone into a common experience. A sense of spontaneous sociability, love for each other, and a sense of solidarity and equality is felt. We have heard "the music" with our heart. This experience molds a vision for the future.

To open our heart, we must somehow to be ready to let go of at least some of our inhibiting perceptions of the mind, so that the music has an entryway to expose us to what is beyond all experiences.

What touches our heart in Playback Theatre is the respect for the mystery of life, which can shine through in every moment or story told. Playback Theatre is a show that helps us not forget how precious life is and that there is a future.

In the worldwide movement of Playback Theatre we must be ready and willing to go through and to overcome crises. The consciousness of the basic values will guide us through times when we might be frustrated, where we get stubborn again and want to be rigid and right, where we are afraid that all is lost.

To let go of the known structures and find new, more accurate ones will only be possible, if we are conscious about the process. In the creative zone we are ready to listen, to trust our individual and collective creativity. What changes us most is what throws us out of our learned behavior and what calls forth hope.

Playback Theatre can bring us closer to peace. We don't demonstrate on the street. We just do our job. We listen to stories and play them back. By doing so, a smooth shift takes place.

We move from the individual to the collective. We start with the personal story to reach the transpersonal. At the end there is "the music," deep inside, ready to spread out.

Playback Theatre is in its own way a peace-building theatre and respects the longing for reconciliation within ourselves and among humans as a community.

Can't we say that Playback Theatre is genius?

AFTERWORD

The center of the heart of us all (not physical heart) is a powerful generator, which can reach far further out than the energies of our physical body. Its energy waves are our pathway to finding resonance in the outside.

This resonating system leaves its mark and creates our life.

The urge for connection – in any possible form – is a basic drive of being human.

The feeling of love is the fastest and most powerful transmitter of energy. We don't do this. It is simply a flow of energy. It just reaches out and tries to connect. That's all. We long for a response, for a caring touch of our heart, for togetherness.

Playback Theatre has its foundation in the knowledge of this central life force.

The world, for the most part, is ruled by rigid minds, and the longing for connection is sometimes hidden by a cloud of frustration or fear. We may even forget about it.

But, the center of our humanity, pulsing in the heart, is pushing towards living. It activates, according to the law of resonance, the energy to connect, to live life and to feel the longing.

It is in this space where Playback Theatre can pick us up. Here is resonance. Here is something calling forth trust instead of fear. Here is an ear for everyone, a smile towards life and a serious nonverbal sharing. In Playback Theatre there is a wideness felt, a world of care and connection, which allows each human being's heart to express itself through story-telling, listening and watching.

I am not sure that Jonathan Fox had in mind that "Playback Theatre leads from the personal to the transpersonal" when he got into developing and creating this theatre.

When he picked those sentences and citations out of hundreds of books and called them, "Some Quotes on Basic Values of Playback Theatre," he expressed the value of what he experienced with this theatre and at the same time what he wanted it to become.

He said it in his incomparable way, and he presented us images and phrases which made us think and explore!

It made Markus and me think, and it helped us to explore Playback Theatre with much excitement.

You have been joining us now on our long walk with many detours, on our excursion into the "Quotes."

At the end of our deep exploration, for me, there is one question remaining: "How do we bring it in?"

How can we put guiding words to this commonality within the expanding movement of Playback Theatre? How can we not forget where the vision wants to lead us? How much do we need to let go, so perfection won't take over, reducing the loving imperfection?

For me "Some Quotes on Basic Values of Playback Theatre," can be the words that guide us all in a common direction.

The quotes, which Jonathan Fox found to be of value, can provide the words beyond our sense of "self," to guide us so we all are able to bring this precious gift to its fullest potential: a theatre for the good of all.

The outcome of our adventure is: The gold of Playback Theatre is worth acquiring!

When Jonathan reads what I had to write down, he may smile.

I hope he smiles.

For me, his smile would express: "I am so glad Playback Theatre is in my life!"

Also, I smile because: "I am so happy Playback Theatre is in my life!"

And also Markus smiles ....

My book is a form of worship and of my deep respect for Playback Theatre.

I see the beauty. I see the potential of Playback Theatre as bridge between different cultures, different countries, different human beings, different ways of perceiving life, and different values of people. A bridge is not meant to erase differences, but to offer connection. Playback Theatre has all the ingredients to create a loving space where we can connect to a "music" beyond. They are the threads that move us from the personal to the transpersonal.

THE LAST STORY

A golden ball is passed on – originated by Jonathan Fox through Playback Theatre – which enriches human beings and the world.

In each story told and played back is a kernel of wisdom, some part of you and of me, about life. This consciousness is worth gold. This gold we pass on.... and on..... and it aggrandizes!

Those golden balls also look like stars popping up in the sky. There are new stars on the sky, all over the world.

The basic values of Playback Theatre will strengthen the connection to and the longing for each other. Between the stars there still may be gaps. But, the energy consisting of the fundamental concept and the awareness of our common base will reduce their effect and can help us to move beyond those gaps.

To be part of Playback Theatre's vision and to be in the middle of its happening is unique and always somehow magical. It is fun and is a challenge, because playing our part means finding our natural intelligence, anchoring our roots in a ground of respect, taking true responsibility in our hands and developing the wings of creativity to fly. To be in the middle of the happening with an open heart lets us experience the mystery of life.

Each one sings its own tune, but together we create a symphony of more joy. A new vibe will create a concert we are all engaged in. Its title might be peace.

And there will be silence: the open space for hope.

This is the stage of Playback Theatre!

It is a space which has something sacred, in which a precious form of common humanness can find expression and can take shape.

It is by our actions on stage that the gold will shine through – the alchemical process of bringing the inside out, feeling comfortable and connected to this world and truly existing in our unique life.

The last story is that the last story is not told yet!

END

THE LAST CANDY

These last pages are an add-on for playbackers. We want to have a look at the structure and to list some of the rules on stage and generally in Playback Theatre. We want to 'remember' and to capture their importance.

Structure and Rules in Practice

The whole structure of Playback Theatre is built up carefully and wisely to provide a space for the team on stage to be able to cooperate smoothly and for the audience to be encouraged to share life experiences without shame or fear.

Since we want to serve, we need to become a free flowing team, composed of actors like creative artists, conductors like shamans and musicians like vibrating vessels.

The differentiated exploration and description of the structure and important rules will help us to swing with the spirit of Playback Theatre.

Structure

By exploring the structure, we found five different subjects worth to look at: dialogue, time and space, cycle, focus, rules.

Dialogue

The conductor's dialogue structures the whole process of a performance.

The conductor is a facilitator whose dialogue with the audience has the focus to make it easy to tell personal experiences. He is encouraging, sometimes challenging, and sometimes humorous. He radiates caring and it is like he is holding his hand out, welcoming what needs and wants to be shared and told.

The length of the dialogue between the conductor and the audience varies, depending on the process within a performance.

His dialogue with the teller brings the story into a clear form, is "private" and supportive. He is like a guide and a friend.

While listening to the dialogue, the actors (and the musician) get their needed information for their following actions.

With his dialogue and his multilayer presence, the conductor maintains connection, the outer frame and ensures the ritual.

Time and space

We have a structure of time and space in Playback Theatre.

As in life itself, each event in life has a beginning, a middle and an ending. So must our performance, our rehearsal, the dialogue and each moment, pair or story played back. This structure in Playback Theatre leaves no open ends, and no endless scenes are played back. Each action gets its time, but no more.

The space available in Playback Theatre (audience and stage) is also structured.

Each party has its own space.

The audience has its own space and sits opposite the stage. The conductor has his space mostly in front stage, since he is the intermediary and is in dialogue with the audience. He must be seen from all and he must be in connection to all. The space of the actors starts in the back where the boxes are. They use the whole stage for the playing back, but return after each play to the back, standing in front of or sitting on the boxes. This says: We are ready for what is coming next. The musician's space is on the left in front, opposite the conductor. He normally stays there, because he has his own set of instruments and can therefore not move. From this place he is in nonverbal interaction with the conductor and the actors. He can be seen from the audience.

For the audience it is easy to capture this division of space.

Cycle

The cycle comprises four steps and is maintained throughout the whole performance: ask a question, answer the question, perform an action, and express appreciation.

First, the conductor asks for a personal experience. Second, someone from the audience, called the teller, answers. Third, the actors play back what the teller has been telling, supported by the musician. Forth, the conductor thanks the teller for sharing a personal experience.

This cycle will be repeated with every moment, pair or story told.

Focus

A performance is built up slowly. It is always an organic process, but its buildup is logical.

In this process the conductor normally asks three types of questions:

1) looking for moments, 2) looking for pairs, and 3) looking for stories.

Mostly we start with moments, move to pairs and than to stories. We move from short narratives to longer ones. Or, very simply said, we move from one feeling to two feelings and then to multiple feelings. This allows the audience to slowly go deeper and to be able to express more about their personal experiences.

1) Moments: Asking for one moment means asking for a feeling, a condition, an impression, or a situation within somebody's life. It is an experience, which is mostly told in few words or sentences.

The look into moments brings forward the fun of telling and of looking at personal experiences. Sitting and watching in the audience, we get curious and "we want more."

Personal moments give everybody a glance into the spectrum of feelings in different situations or into one aspect of somebody's inner life. Telling only a personal moment and feeling seems rather easy.

Asking for moments at the beginning is our way to be gentle and careful with our audience. The moment is played back in a moment! At the same time it is a warm up for more and longer narratives.

Moments are often played back as short forms, mostly for example as the so-called "fluid sculpture:" a sculpture that moves, makes sounds, can speak and can have different aspects. In the presentation normally are no persons or objects in action, nor is there dialogue between the actors. It is only the expressed feeling of the moment of the teller, played back in movement and sound. Fluid sculptures have a great potential: short and strong, personal and clear. There are also transformative fluid sculptures: we flow from one feeling to the next to demonstrate a change of feelings in this particular moment.

2) Pairs: After looking at some moments, often pairs will follow.

We ask for something like "two voices in the head," "two souls in the chest," or "two feelings concerning a decision or a situation."

Pairs are the expression of ambivalence or an inner conflict. Pairs can express an inside struggle or touch an existential base.

They are more complex than moments. They often reach into a deeper level of our personality.

We don't know their background, and therefore we let them simply appear on stage as part of human experiences, played back in a short sequence. But we know by their appearance that we have touched other subjects. We allow deeper levels to be here, but only by touching on them briefly.

Pairs are played back by two actors simultaneously, each taking one side of the ambivalence to make its tension visible.

Pairs are a further step and show another part of us, more of the inside world, and the challenges we face in life. They are not only a new experience for the audience, but also a transition that takes us into full stories.

3) Stories: Sometime later the conductor moves to stories. The moments and pairs told before have already called forth stories laying beyond them. People are not only more ready to tell stories, but they also feel the excitement to do so and are comfortable with the way their narrative are handled by the team. Trust and courage makes them ready to tell more personal experiences. It is more easy now to come on stage to tell them.

Stories are the expression of all human experiences, as we have discovered in quote one. Their playing back is longer and wider. They are "real theatre pieces."

People, objects and all kinds of roles will now appear on stage. Stories take us to different places, homes and scenery, and introduce a large variety of feelings.

The invisible connections among people will get stronger, because there are a lot of possibilities to project and connect. There is more time to let ourselves journey deeper into the vibes of a story.

Many different forms have been created for playing back stories. We are listing only a few here:

a) Scenes:

The teller chooses all the different roles and the story is played back according to the dynamics of the story, or the teller chooses only one role, an actor for himself.

I am firmly convinced, that the teller must have a presence on stage. The teller must have a mirror!

To have an actor "being me," is an intimate action, which is psychologically so important. As teller we "put ourselves in somebody else's hands," and we have some tension about how we will be represented. If there is a "me" on stage, an actor who can role-reverse with me, then there is someone here, who can understand me, who can find words for me and for whatever has happened to me. This can be so releasing! The teller's actor is like our confidant!

We feel seen, and this is what we all need so badly, if we want to admit it or not. In Playback Theatre we are treated with respect and compassion. To feel understood, "not alone," and "not crazy or abnormal" makes us ready to look at ourselves more lovingly and more clearly. By looking at myself on stage, there can be these moments of insights without judgment.

b) the actors split the story into sequences

c) the story can be played back as an opera, 'mosaic' or 'tableau,'

d) and as all those wonderful possibilities which have been created.

There are a variety of beautiful forms to play back a story. The ultimate 'form' would be to have no form!

The choice of the form depends on the skills of the team and their creativity.

Of course we always create new forms in our rehearsals according to our creative process and fun, but only a few will be transferred into a repertoire valid for all.

The forms which have been developed by Jonathan Fox's original company are used all over the world. The 'known forms' bring a smooth and creative flow into the joint acting of playbackers from different countries, cultures and languages.

Rules

We first want to have a quick and incomplete foray into the word rule.

We have to remember that most rules came out of a need. The origin of a rule was a desire for the better or a worthwhile attempt for doing something differently. Rules are meant to help us live together; for structure, safety and clarity instead of confusion.

But what happened to these originally meaningful rules? What have we humans done with all the rules? We use them as instruments for power. We make money with them. We fight over them. We try to cheat to avoid adhering to them. We are afraid that we are losing our personal freedom, and this fear evokes resistance. We resist following rules that tell us we "have to."

In Playback Theatre we never would ask trainees to follow rules out of an imaginary required obedience, because their actions would immediately miss spontaneity, power and vibe.

Our rules are actually guidelines that provide clarity in our actions on stage. They help the actors to feel free and comfortable. They provide security. We want an uninterrupted flow of energy throughout this exciting process. The rules make it easy, and they make so much sense!

Rules for moments or pairs

The actors are standing while listening.

The teller stays sitting in the audience.

Before acting, there is this important "in-between step!"

It is this one step forward that enables us to change from ourselves into a feeling. It makes the action on stage transparent and clear. Mostly the joint action ends like a frozen statue. Then the actors unfreeze and, with a look back to the teller, their action is complete. The step backwards follows. Then they stand still until the next "in-between step" for the next playback.

Space, as a generally important element on stage concerning clarity and artistry, also helps us to transform: here I am myself, there I am "this."

In pairs, this step happens when the two actors get ready to stand together. This gives them the needed space for their action.

Both are either facing the audience or standing back-to-back, moving like a merry-go-round. Like that, everybody can feel the two inside parts. There is no interaction. We want to see the tension! Depending on the number of actors, a pair told can be shown in different variations by two other actors.

Rules for stories from start to end

Since stories are not short forms, there are more steps to go.

There are eight main steps to consider for stories:

A) "Warming up:" The conductor is in dialogue with the audience and a teller arises.

To tell a story, the teller needs to come 'on stage.' The conductor invites him to take seat on his left side on the "teller's chair," between him and the actors. This is the most 'safe' place for him: near the actors (who will play back his personal story and from whom he will choose the characters), and under the protection of the conductor, so he doesn't feel so exposed suddenly sitting in front of all. He can feel comfortable telling his story and the conductor can have a "private" encounter with him. The actors sit on their boxes.

B) "Interview:" The teller tells a personal story, developed and shaped with the help of the conductor. The actors, engaged in listening, stand up when chosen for a role. They are not asking or speaking during the interview.

C) "Pass–over:" The conductor ends the interview and passes the story over to the actors and the musician with the magical words "Lets watch!"

D) "Setting up:" The actors, without words or planning, prepare the space and themselves for the story to be played back, while the musician is playing some music. When the actors are ready, he stops and the enactment can begin.

E) "Playing back:" During the playback of a story, the conductor and the teller are silently watching, without interrupting or talking. The scene must have a clear ending. The actors stand still for a moment, looking at the teller, as if they would give the story "back to him" with their eyes.

F) "Check back:" Feedback from the teller. The conductor asks the teller if the playback captured something of his story. The teller answers this question.

If there is a need for another ending, the new ending will be acted out and another check-back with the teller will follow.

G) "Honoring:" The conductor thanks the teller for sharing a personal experience.

H) "End:" The teller leaves his seat on stage, and goes back to his place or chair in the audience.

Sometimes, it's not so easy to keep the structure in place.

We can be challenged as conductor, as it happened once to Jim.

"We wanted to introduce Playback Theatre in the countryside, at a place which had become a new cultural center. We were invited to perform. The mayor promised to come. The audience was not familiar with this kind of theatre. For us it was a great chance to present Playback Theatre in a new area. After some fluid sculptures and pairs, I introduced 'the two chairs' and asked for the first story. Immediately, a man got up. John came on stage and said, "I don't want to sit on the chair and tell, I want to sing a song." As a conductor I wanted to stick to the structure, but at the same time I didn't want to frustrate the first enthusiastic teller. Many things went through my head: "Will I weaken my role as a conductor if I allow singing? Is it good to take a risk? What will the audience think about that? What will happen next, after the singing?" Finally, I suggested: "OK, first you sing, and then you will tell us your story about this song." He accepted and started with his song. It was a love song about watching a beautiful woman who is playing a flute under a tree and thinking about her unfulfilled life. Well, during his song, he started to walk through the audience, finally singing his song to a woman who was sitting beside his chair in the audience. At the end he came back on stage and wanted to caress my cheek. I tried to hold his hand back, because I didn't want to be caressed. I was surprised about my own reaction; his behavior made me nervous. How to go on? I invited John on the tellers chair, which he first refused. I reminded him of our deal, but John wanted to sit on the conductors chair. At that moment it felt like a never-ending challenge. I decided not to give up the position as conductor – and with it my chair – and suggested: "You can sit on the chair next to the audience, but first let's change the chairs." I took my chair and let him sit on 'his' (the teller's chair) on my right side. At least I found some way out without getting in a fight. Then John told his story. The song was about falling in love with a woman: the woman sitting in the audience. After the story was told, John told the actors that wanted to see his story in some kind of ancient song-lines – as he was using in his song. The actors enacted the story in their own way, without being annoyed by John's demand. The woman in the audience smiled.

In the gathering with the audience after the show, some people mentioned the first storytelling. Some playbackers said to me that they would have rejected John, or wouldn't have tolerated his behavior. Somebody asked if this situation was arranged beforehand, and someone else said that John was crazy. For me, as a conductor, it was a difficult situation. I thought a lot about it afterward, and learned a lot!"

This story brings up another subject concerning rules:

Rules for our Planning

Jonathan Fox once talked about the planning of performances, as another task and challenge of the conductor, to maintain structure and to create a space in which community spirit can grow.

A) The context, the concept, time and place must match.

Our planning as conductors must include some important questions and considerations, which should be checked out before an event is taking place. Some of the questions to ask can be: "Where does the performance take place?" or "What is the background of this performance?" If it is part of a bigger event: "Is the timing correct?" and "What are the expectations?"

B) The conductor and the group have to know what focus they have and where their limitations are.

C) Trust and a community spirit are obligatory.

D) Playback Theatre has a concept of "democracy – hierarchy" or "freedom – order." We need hierarchy to keep the ritual going as it is supposed to, and we need democracy to carry it through together.

E) The conductor is somebody who is a real leader.

F) The actors do not play back one-to-one. It is more.

G) Transparency is important to permit the letting go into Playback Theatre's ritual.

H) An inner attitude of respect is needed to deal in an appropriate way with personal experiences.

'Remember:' Structure and rules are manifestations of the inherent spirit of Playback Theatre and they make it easy for all to enter into a space, where a community can grow and transformation can happen.

REFERENCES

Eichler, Norbert A. (1983): Das Buch der Wirklichkeit

Fox, Jonathan (1986): Theatre of Love (self-pulished)

Fox, Jonathan (1994): Acts of Service. Spontaneity, Commitment, Tradition in the Nonscipted Theatre. New Paltz, NY

Fox, Jonathan/ Dauber, Heinrich (Hrsg.) (1999): Playbacktheater – wo Geschichten sich begegnen. Internationale Beiträge zu Theorie und Praxis des Playbacktheaters. Klinkhardt

Frankl, Victor E. (1997): Man's search for meaning

Gelman, Rita G. (2002): Tales of a female nomad

Henne, Annette/ Huehn, Markus (2003): Die Vision des Playback Theaters (audiobook, self-published)

Jung, Carl G.: Gesammelte Werke

Laotze: Tao Te King. Übers. Hanspeter Kindler

Mares, Theun (1998): The Mists of Dragon Lore. Lionheart Publishing CC

Moreno, Jakob L. (1974): Die Grundlagen der Soziometrie

Ruiz, Don Miguel (1997): The 4 agreements

Ruiz, Don Miguel (1999): The Mastery of Love

Salas, Jo (1993): Improvising Real Life. Personal Story in Playback Theatre.

Dubuque / Iowa / USA

Samdu, Lama Kazi Dawa (1995): Das Tibetanische Totenbuch

Sams, Jamie (1990): The discovery of self through native teachings. Sacred Path Cards

Sheldrake, Rupert (2003): Das Gedächtnis der Natur

Wilber, Ken (1996): Eros, Kosmos, Logos

References Fox
Bellah, Robert et. al. (1985): Habits of the Heart
Boal, Augusto (1979): Theatre of the Oppressed
Bohm, David (1996): On Dialogue
Coles, Robert (1989): The Call of Stories
Freire, Paulo (1973): Education for Critical Consciousness
Grotowski, Jerzy (1968): Towards a Poor Theater
Hunniger, (1955): The Origin of Theatre
Maritain, Jacques (1968): Integral Humanism
Moreno, Jacob Levy (1937): Who Shall Survive
Moreno, Jacob Levy (1947): Theater of Spontaneity
Neihardt, John (1932): Black Elk Speaks
Paley, Vivian (1986): Mollie is Three: Growing Up in School
Tillich, Paul (1954): The Courage to Be
Turner, Victor (1974): Dramas, Fields, and Metaphors
Turner, Victor (1981): From Ritual to Theatre; the Human Seriousness of Play
Vanier, Jean (1993): Community & Growth
West, Cornel (1993): Race Matters

Web: 05/2012 – 06/2013
http://www.sacred-texts.com/cdshop/index.htm
http://oxforddictionaries.com
https://www.e-education.psu.edu/astro801/content/l2_p5.html
http://www.crystalinks.com/pythagoras.html
http://www.crystalinks.com/astronomy.html
http://www.crystalinks.com/musicspheres.html
http://www.sacred-texts.com/eso/sta/sta19.htm
http://www.aboutscotland.com/harmony/prop.html
http://www.pythagoras-institut.de/Institut/Klang/Musik/index.html

It was only one page...

Some Quotes On Basic Values Of Playback Theatre

by Jonathan Fox

We all have a [worthwhile] story

"You can't forget the stories, and you think about them not only here, when we're talking about them, but in your car, or when you're walking, or when you're out there doing your work." Coles, The Call of Stories, 1989

"The courage to be is the courage to accept oneself as accepted in spite of being unacceptable." Tillich, The Courage to Be, 1952

A bond exists between "communitas, liminality, and lowermost status." Turner, Dramas, Fields, and Metaphors, 1974

As a community we are wise

"Knowledge is not extended from those who consider they know to those who consider that they do not know. Knowledge is built up in relations between human beings and the world." Paolo Freire, Education,

"I suggest that the movement towards coherence is innate, but our thought has muddled it." Bohm, On Dialogue, 1996

"Communities...have a history--in an important sense t hey are constituted by their past--and for this reason we can speak of a real community as a 'community of memory,' one that does not forget its past. In order not to forget that past, a community is involved in retelling its story, its constitutive narrative, and in so doing, it offers examples..." Bellah, et. al., Habits of the Heart, 1985.

Everyone is a [creative] actor

"Art is immanent to all men, and not only to a select few; art is not to be sold, no more than are breathing, thinking, loving. Art is not merchandise. Boal, Theatre of the Oppressed, 1979

"Place this three-year-old in a room with other threes and sooner or later they will become an acting company, Paley, Mollie is Three: Growing Up in School, 1986

Boal writes about practicing "simultaneous dramaturgy" active involvement of the audience during course of play. Boal, Theatre of the Oppressed, 1979

"The audience theatre is a community theater. It is the community from which the dramas spring and the actors producing them, and again it is not any community, a community in abstracto, but our village and neighborhood, the house in which we live. The actors are not any people, people in abstracto, but our people, our fathers and mothers, our brothers and sisters, our friends and neighbors." Moreno, Theater of Spontaneity. 1947

"Ours then is a via negativa--not a collection of skills, but an eradication of blocks.", Grotowski, Towards a Poor Theater, 1968

Community spirit [and a mood of positive participation] is transformational

"The problem is how to elicit from every man his maximum spontaneous participation." Moreno, Who Shall Survive, 1937

"A love ethic has nothing to do with sentimental feelings or tribal connections. Rather it is a last attempt at generating a sense of agency among a downtrodden people." West, Race Matters, 1993

We can connect to a "music" beyond our immediate concerns that will bring peace and joy

"When I visit communities, I frequently ask, 'How do you celebrate?' If they say, 'We don't celebrate,' then I know the community risks death." Vanier, Community & Growth, 1993,

A person is "transversed by the solicitations of actual grace." Maritain, Integral Humanism, 1968

"The dance ritual was a means of entering the Unseen by force: a two-way contact with the divine, both persuading and being inspired." Hunniger, The Origin of Theatre, 1955

"When the ceremony was over, everybody felt a great deal better, for it had been a day of fun. They were better able now to see the greenness of the world, the wideness of the sacred day, the colours of the earth." Neihardt, Black Elk Speaks, 1932

Not classes, "culture circles; "not pupils, "group participants; not lecture, "dialogue." Freire, Education for Critical Consciousness, 1973

Turner uses term "liminal " to refer to the "creative zone " in the social drama when the rules are in limbo. What happens in the liminal state is a future" Turner, From Ritual to Theatre: the Human Seriousness of Play, 1981

remembering

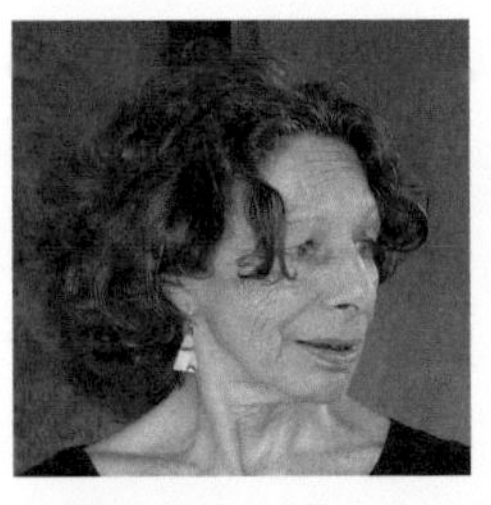

Annette Henne was born in Switzerland at the end of the Second World War. She is now retired and lives in Bali, Indonesia.
As a child Annette loved to act out different characters – and she was always an attentive listener to the experiences and stories of the people around her. Theatre and psychology naturally became part of her adult life and later she became a psychotherapist. In her practice, she was influenced by C.G. Jung's Analytical Psychology, J.L. Moreno's psychodrama, Native American teachings and Transpersonal Psychology.
In 1986 Annette propitiously came upon Playback Theatre. It was like a magical door to an art form that offers the fascinating combination of playing, theatre, applied psychology and transpersonality that can be used to benefit humanity.
She was the one who brought Playback Theatre to German speaking Europe.

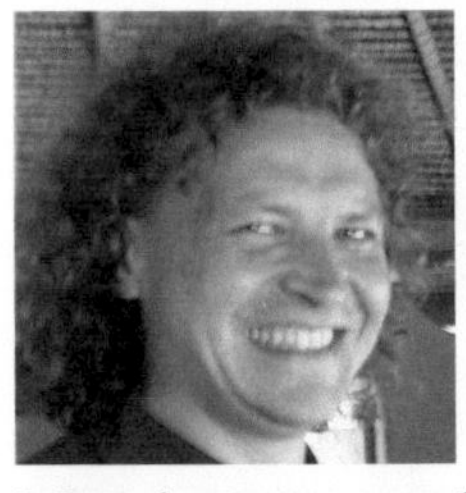

Markus Huehn was born in Germany 1969, lives in Germany and is a courageous self-employed man. Markus Huehn has a wide spectrum to offer for grown ups and children. He is engaged in social activities, including theatre at schools, theatre with disabled, and circus performances with children. His workshops are uniquely created for each event.
Most important to his study educational science, was the awareness of the missing piece in society and schools: creative play and the benefit by interacting.
Markus is not only a passionate playbacker since 1996 - he is also gifted clown.
To him Playback Theatre captures the need for seriousness, humour and heart in today's world.

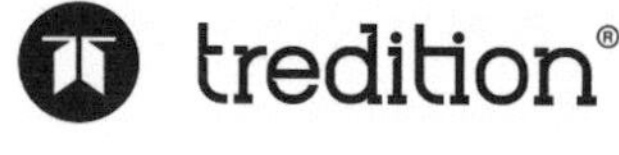

www.tredition.de

Über tredition

Der tredition Verlag wurde 2006 in Hamburg gegründet. Seitdem hat tredition Hunderte von Büchern veröffentlicht. Autoren können in wenigen leichten Schritten print-Books, e-Books und audio-Books publizieren. Der Verlag hat das Ziel, die beste und fairste Veröffentlichungsmöglichkeit für Autoren zu bieten.

tredition wurde mit der Erkenntnis gegründet, dass nur etwa jedes 200. bei Verlagen eingereichte Manuskript veröffentlicht wird. Dabei hat jedes Buch seinen Markt, also seine Leser. tredition sorgt dafür, dass für jedes Buch die Leserschaft auch erreicht wird

Autoren können das einzigartige Literatur-Netzwerk von tredition nutzen. Hier bieten zahlreiche Literatur-Partner (das sind Lektoren, Übersetzer, Hörbuchsprecher und Illustratoren) ihre Dienstleistung an, um Manuskripte zu verbessern oder die Vielfalt zu erhöhen. Autoren vereinbaren unabhängig von tredition mit Literatur-Partnern die Konditionen ihrer Zusammenarbeit und können gemeinsam am Erfolg des Buches partizipieren.

Das gesamte Verlagsprogramm von tredition ist bei allen stationären Buchhandlungen und Online-Buchhändlern wie z. B. Amazon erhältlich. e-Books stehen bei den führenden Online-Portalen (z. B. iBook-Store von Apple) zum Verkauf.

Seit 2009 bietet tredition sein Verlagskonzept auch als sogenanntes "White-Label" an. Das bedeutet, dass andere Personen oder Institutionen risikofrei und unkompliziert selbst zum Herausgeber von Büchern und Buchreihen unter eigener Marke werden können.

Mittlerweile zählen zahlreiche renommierte Unternehmen, Zeitschriften-, Zeitungs- und Buchverlage, Universitäten, Forschungseinrichtungen, Unternehmensberatungen zu den Kunden von tredition. Unter www.tredition-corporate.de bietet tredition vielfältige weitere Verlagsleistungen speziell für Geschäftskunden an.

tredition wurde mit mehreren Innovationspreisen ausgezeichnet, u. a. Webfuture Award und Innovationspreis der Buch-Digitale.

tredition ist Mitglied im Börsenverein des Deutschen Buchhandels.